The *Church T*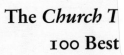
100 Best

The *Church Times* Book of 100 Best Prayers

Edited and compiled by
Rachel Boulding

CANTERBURY
PRESS
Norwich

British Library Cataloguing in Publication data

A catalogue record for this book is available
from the British Library

ISBN 1-85311-678-5/9781 85311 678 0

Typeset by Regent Typesetting, London
Printed and bound in Great Britain by
William Clowes Ltd, Beccles, Suffolk

Contents

Acknowledgements   vi

Notes on contributors   vii

Introduction: Prayer by Sister Wendy Beckett   I

God's presence   4

Creation   22

Joy   30

Faith   38

Worship   52

Calling   64

Wisdom and justice   86

Peace   104

Darkness and sin   112

Pilgrimage and perseverance   128

Death   162

Hope   172

Advent and Christmas   182

Easter   194

Sources and acknowledgements   204

Index of authors of prayers   206

Acknowledgements

The prayers and commentaries in this book are all drawn from the *Prayer for the week* column in the *Church Times*. They are a selection from the contributions that have appeared since the column began in May 2003.

I would like to thank for their help in preparing the text: Eleanor Handley, Helen Keddie, Jim Nagel, and, at Canterbury Press, Mary Matthews, Christine Smith and Jenny Willis.

Rachel Boulding, Deputy Editor, *Church Times*

Notes on contributors

Canon David Adam, the retired Vicar of Lindisfarne, is the author of more than 20 books on spirituality, beginning with *The Edge of Glory* (Triangle/SPCK, 1985).

Sister Wendy Beckett is a hermit, art critic, and the author of many books.

The Revd John Burniston is Vicar of St Martin's, Heaton, Bradford, and the Bishop's adviser in liturgy for the diocese of Bradford.

The Revd Georgina Byrne is Vicar of St Kenelm's, Romsley, in the Halas Team, in the diocese of Worcester.

The Revd Dr Lorraine Cavanagh is the Anglican chaplain for Cardiff University.

The Rt Revd John D. Davies was Bishop of Shrewsbury from 1987 to 1994. He worked in South Africa from 1956 to 1970.

Prebendary John Gaskell is a retired Vicar of St Alban's, Holborn, London, and a founder of Affirming Catholicism.

Dr Paula Gooder teaches at the Queen's Foundation, Birmingham, and is a freelance lecturer in biblical studies.

The Revd Dr Joanne Woolway Grenfell is part-time Priest-in-Charge in Manor Ecumenical Parish, Sheffield.

The Revd Dr Cally Hammond is Dean of Gonville and Caius College, Cambridge.

Jamie Hawkey is training for the priesthood at Westcott House, and is a Gosden Scholar of Selwyn College, Cambridge.

The Revd Nicholas Holtam is Vicar of St Martin-in-the-Fields, London.

Kenneth Macnab teaches RE at the Oratory School, near Reading.

The Revd Melvyn Matthews is Canon Emeritus of Wells Cathedral, where he served as Chancellor before his retirement in 2005. He is the author of *Both Alike to Thee* (SPCK, 2000) and *Nearer than Breathing* (SPCK, 2002).

The Revd J. Philip Newell, the former Warden of Iona Abbey, is a Church of Scotland minister, and the author of many books, including *Celtic Treasure* (Canterbury Press, 2005).

The Revd Emma Percy is Chaplain of Trinity College, Oxford.

The Rt Revd John Pritchard is the Bishop of Jarrow and the author of *How to Pray* (SPCK, 2002) and *Living Easter through the Year* (SPCK, 2005).

The Revd Annabel Shilson-Thomas is a priest in the diocese of Ely, and spirituality materials consultant at CAFOD.

The Rt Revd David Silk is a retired Bishop of Ballarat, Australia.

The Revd Mark Speeks is Assistant Priest at St James's, West Hampstead, and St Mary's, Kilburn, London.

James Walters is a former parliamentary researcher training for ordination at Westcott House, and is a Gosden Scholar of Selwyn College, Cambridge.

The Revd David Warbrick is the Vicar of St Giles's, Packwood, with St Thomas's, Hockley Heath, in the diocese of Birmingham.

The Revd Dr Robin Ward is Vicar of St John's, Sevenoaks, and Canon Theologian of Rochester Cathedral.

The Revd Martin Warner is Canon Pastor of St Paul's Cathedral.

The Revd Dr Jo Bailey Wells was Tutor in Old Testament at Ridley Hall, Cambridge, and is now Director of Anglican Studies and Associate Professor of the Practice of Ministry and Bible at Duke University, Northern Carolina.

The Revd Dr Sam Wells was formerly Vicar of St Mark's, Cambridge, and is now Dean of Chapel and Research Professor in Christian Ethics at Duke University, Northern Carolina.

Dr Alan Wilson is the Bishop of Buckingham.

Introduction
Prayer by Sister Wendy Beckett

If you are a Christian, you want to pray: it is of the essence, the spontaneous result of believing in the real God. This is the God that Jesus reveals to us – no strong, punitive judge, but a Father so fatherly that St Paul can say that from him 'all fatherhood' takes its name.

God is absolute Father, all love, all support, all guidance: how could anyone who truly believed in him not pray, not want to pray? But 'want' has two meanings. It can mean 'desire', long, in the sense of the psalmist's 'longing and yearning'. At this definition, you may feel inclined to groan, and think that on these terms you are not up to scratch. (There is a strange but persistent delusion that everybody else knows how to pray, but that you have somehow missed the secret.) There are people who know this passionate desire for prayer, but that is their good fortune. The desire that is natural to one who believes is a desire of will, a choice, not necessarily felt with intensity.

The difference is clear if we think of temptation. You may feel a deep emotional desire to do something that you know is wrong, but your deeper desire (please God), is to do what is right, what is in keeping with the mind of Christ. All the feeling is on one side and all the acting is on the other. It is in that sense that a Christian wants to pray.

This is even clearer on the other meaning of the word: 'need'. We all need prayer. You will remember how the apostles almost threw up their hands in despair at the demands of following Jesus, and told him bluntly that it was impossible. The Lord did not argue with them; he agreed. 'With men this is impossible; but with God all things are possible' (Matthew 19.26).

God is always there to make things possible, but how can he help us unless we allow him? This turning to our Father is precisely what we mean by prayer. It is something so simple and straightforward, yet so demanding in its implications, that we cannot accept its lack of problems. There is nothing to prayer, except willingness to let God be God to us; to let the Spirit of Jesus love the Father within us. How? By being still before him.

This book is about said prayers, but we cannot say prayers at all unless we know also the prayer of silence. In silent prayer – no words and hence no thoughts – we are still. You remember the old peasant who said of his prayer: 'I looks at him and he looks at me.' The first half of that famous sentence is rather mysterious, since when we look at God we see nothing. It is the second half that matters: 'He looks at me.'

In that looking, God purifies me into goodness, gives me his peace, silently transforms me, little by little, into what he has already destined me to be. The silence is nothing to be afraid of. Five minutes, ten minutes, longer if you have time: we simply hold ourselves out to him for him to take possession.

Thoughts will bustle in – we ignore them (temptations to think it all a waste of time) – we persevere. Even for psychic health, a resting in quiet is therapeutic; the mind is not made for incessant movement. But to know what this rest means, that it is on God's heart that we rest and insensibly draw strength, that is the privilege of the believer. Unless our spoken prayer has this silence at its centre, we can be in danger of that 'too much speaking' of which the heathens were accused (Matthew 6.7). (The implication is that they knew no better.) As you read through this book, it will become very clear that here is not spiritual chatter, or even that pious speculation that substitutes thinking about God to praying to him.

There are certainly many deep and inspiring thoughts here, from a great diversity of sources, but each is a prayer that has a special meaning for the writer. These are lived prayers, prayers that have intertwined themselves into the textures of a life. Some of the contributors explain how these particular prayers have come to be precious to them. Often the association is with people, holy men and women whom this form of words brings to mind. For one author, it is three women: an elderly lady he visited as a boy, a nun, and St Teresa of Avila; for another, it is an old friend, or a character in the scriptures. Or it may be a place, a certain cathedral or church, a graveyard or deathbed, a place in the world that we specially love or find beautiful. It may be a thing, like a piece of pottery, or an event such as the eucharistic celebration, an idea, like the meaning of poverty or the importance of peace. Each writer in this book has found spoken prayers that sum up the depth of some deeply felt experience.

These prayers come from a multitude of sources. There are secular writers, like Tolstoy and Robert Louis Stevenson, there are poets, like Herbert and Donne, there are saints, like St Catherine of Genoa or St Patrick. There are theologians, like Karl Rahner and John Henry Newman. There is a lovely prayer by a marathon runner, one attributed to Francis Drake, several from Jewish sources, others from Africa, Brazil, Russia. Not a few are anonymous, from a wide range of centuries.

But most, of course, come from the liturgy, and this book would be invaluable from that angle alone. The liturgy is our joint prayer, when we all, as God's pilgrim people, stand before him and proclaim his greatness and goodness. The pace has to suit the congregation, and we can slip into the fatal habit of merely saying these prayers, as if all that was needed was presence and voice. But it is our whole selves that the liturgy demands, and a gentle saying of these prayers, slowly to ourselves, will help to make us aware of them when we say them together.

Apart from the prayers that are scriptural quotations, where the light of God is very bright, I love specially the anonymous prayers. Here, some Christian, whom we shall never know, set in words his or her affirmation of God. Nobody can enter into the secret of another's relationship with God; we are not even able to assess our own. But these lovely and living praises and petitions are the fruits of such relationships.

That is something we must never forget. There is no absolute distinction between prayer and action. 'By their fruits you shall know them' (Matthew 7.20). If we pray – that is, if we accept that to be a Christian means to live in God, more or less according to the depth of our faith – then we cannot cease from that relationship when we cease to turn our thoughts to God explicitly. What we do is our prayer in action. If you read one of these pages every day, or one every week, the thoughts you find there should have an effect on your ordinary life: how you speak to your family or how you cope with your problems, or how you get on with your work.

On each page, somebody else is sharing with you a wellspring from which he or she draws holy refreshment, comes closer to God, understands life better, and is supported. Some will speak to you more powerfully than others, but all will certainly speak, if you will let them.

You may well have a best prayer of your own, which rises instinctively to your mind at times. If not, why not find one? As this book shows, the possibilities are infinite. 'The world is full of your riches,' sang the psalmist (Psalm 104.24), and so do we.

God's presence

The light of Christ

Christ as a light,
Illumine and guide me!
Christ as a shield, o'ershadow and cover me!
Christ be under me! Christ be over me!
Christ be beside me,
On left hand and right!
Christ be before me, behind me, about me!
Christ this day, be within and without me!

St Patrick's Breastplate (ascribed to St Patrick, 372–466,
translated by James Clarence Mangan)

<hr/>

This James Clarence Mangan translation of *St Patrick's Breastplate* first appeared in *Duffy's Magazine* and was later printed in Mangan's *Collected Poems* (published in New York in 1859). A more familiar translation of the hymn is Mrs Alexander's 'I bind unto myself today', which was sung at York Minster on St Patrick's Day in 1891, when Archbishop William Magee, an Irishman, was enthroned. Sadly, this hymn is now missing from many of our hymnbooks.

I have taught this prayer to school and pilgrim groups visiting Holy Island. I called it 'The Prayer of Seven Directions'. I prefer to give it a more flowing movement, making an encircling prayer of it: Christ before me, on my right, behind me, on my left, beneath me, above me – and within me.

I encouraged children to act it out. I made sure they understood they were not making Christ come; rather, they were opening their lives to Christ, who ever comes to them.

We began by facing the east, the place of the rising sun, the start of the day. Christ before me: at the beginning of the day, at the beginning of any new event, wherever we go, whatever we do, Christ is waiting to meet us. We may not know what lies ahead, but we know who waits for us. Start each day by seeking to meet Christ.

Christ on my right: turning to the south, the direction of the midday sun, Christ is there in the thick of life. Christ is in our work and activity. Christ is present in the fullness of life, in our dexterity and our abilities.

Christ behind me: he is behind us to protect us against our own past. He comes with forgiveness. He can protect us from anything that would sneak up on us to hurt us. He is with us on the sunset road, often un-noticed, but always there.

Christ on my left: now we face the darkness of the north. Christ is present in our darkness and in the darkness of the world. When sinister things happen to us and around us, Christ never leaves us.

Christ beneath me: this is the Christ who descended, who went into the depths of life, who descended into death. He is there to uphold: 'Under-neath are the everlasting arms.' However deep we sink, we will find that he is there.

Christ above me: he who descended also ascended. He came down to lift us up. He died that we might rise, became human that we might share in the divine.

We have now completed six directions. This can be expressed in the words: 'We are in the heart of God.' Once we know that God is greater than we are, and that we cannot fully contain him, we can say: 'Christ within me.'

I like children to point at themselves as they say these words, then to acknowledge that Christ is in each of us. We are called to see Christ in others, and to be Christ to others. Let Christ work within us. Let us respect the Christ in others.

David Adam

Love beyond words

O sweet and loving God,
when I stay asleep too long,
oblivious to all your many blessings,
then, please, wake me up,
and sing to me your joyful song.
It is a song without noise or notes.
It is a song of love beyond words,
of faith beyond the power of human telling.
I can hear it in my soul
when you awaken me
to your presence.

Mechthild of Magdeburg (1210–80)

There is a wonderful vibrancy and immediacy to Mechthild of Magdeburg's prayer. Known for *The Flowing Light of the Godhead*, a series of seven books she wrote over three decades, she is one of the very few medieval female voices. Mechthild lived most of her life as a Beguine.

Seen by the Church as suspect, although long tolerated, the Beguines were a spontaneous movement of religious women, with no Rule, no constitution, no vows, and no cloister. They lived in autonomous communities, and were known for their charitable activities, devotion to the eucharist, and a mysticism that combined a belief in the union of the human soul with God and medieval notions of courtly love.

While we can see many of the elements of Beguine spirituality in Mechthild's prayer, which echoes the texture of the Song of Songs – from the intimacy of spiritual union to the courtly use of song – it is strikingly modern. It has an air of spiritual liberty that may be challenging to many.

Mechthild is asking God to arouse her from her sleep, to whisper the eternal song of divine love into her ear, and to make her alive to his presence. Praying a love prayer to God that resonates with sexual undercurrents might seem offensive. But how many of us can claim to be in love with God as deeply as Mechthild clearly is?

In her prayer, God is being asked to be nothing more than God. This prayer is no supplication for help in a current distress: there is no wanting God to change circumstances or forgive past errors. God is asked to provide only his presence. There is no guilt nor shame, no subservience nor self-belittlement. There is nothing tortured about Mechthild's prayer. It reflects a confidence in and an openness to God: that God, a God of 'love beyond words', will raise her up to meet him on an almost equal footing.

The prayer tells of a song that has no noise or notes, a song beyond words, a song that is pure silence. It is a silence, nevertheless, that can be heard by the soul. The apparent paradox of a silent song points to God's presence as being the song: the Logos, the Word, providing the noiseless background to all creation. Yet it is a silence that has a spiritual rhythm to which we can attune ourselves.

The prayer also speaks of a faith that is beyond the power of human telling. But this is not Mechthild's faith, nor ours. It is God's faith: a faith in the ultimate goodness of his creation and in the ultimate goodness of each one of us. The prayer is about God's faith and love in Mechthild – a faith and a love that are so intense that Mechthild resents sleep.

Little is heard of God's faith in us. Perhaps the Church's history of emphasizing our unworthiness before God prevents us from seeing faith as being two-way. As children of God, by God's design, we are worthy not only of being loved, but also of God having faith in us.

At its core, Mechthild's prayer is about the dignity of being human. It is about taking on our full stature before God – just as we are. For Mechthild, union with God is not oblivion in God, however loving, but an eternal love-dance.

Mark Speeks

Blessing

The Lord bless you
   and keep you;
The Lord make his face to shine upon you,
   and be gracious to you;
The Lord lift up his countenance upon you,
   and give you peace.

Numbers 6.24–26 (NRSV)

According to the book of Numbers, these are words that God spoke to Moses for Aaron and his descendants to use in blessing the people of Israel. This is God's prayer for his people – which becomes their prayer for others.

It is a prayer for all time. Its ancient significance is confirmed by an archaeological find in Jerusalem a few years ago. These words were on scrolls in two silver cylinders discovered in burial caves in Jerusalem dating from 600 BC. That makes them the earliest known fragments of any biblical texts – pre-dating the Dead Sea Scroll manuscripts by about 400 years.

It's so normal for us to end formal worship with a blessing that we might miss its significance. I remember the astonishment of a congregation at a service of induction for a new vicar, when the bishop hesitated before giving the final blessing. He asked them to reflect on what it meant: for themselves, for the incumbent, for the parish, and for God. Only then did he continue with the blessing.

The language here is compact and poetic. The Hebrew consists of three lines, parallel in form and content, and each line contains two clauses. The first clause invokes God's action (to bless, his face to shine, to lift his face), and the second describes the benefits (keep you, be gracious to you, give you peace).

There is a progression in length – from the first line of three words, to the second line of five words, to the third of seven words – mirroring the outward movement of God's blessing from the priest to the gathered community to the world. There is also a progression of intensity – from general well-being to the (passive) shining of God's face, to the (more active) movement of God lifting the face.

The Lord (*Yhwh*) is named as the subject in the first clause of each of the three lines, even though the syntax doesn't require this repetition. Although Aaron and his priestly descendants are charged with voicing the blessing, it is only through Israel's God that blessing occurs.

God's work among his people falls into two modes: salvation and blessing. On the one hand, salvation is manifest through God's particular acts in history – most specifically, at the exodus and in Christ. On the other, blessing describes God's constant unending care in providing and sustaining. These are two contrasting dimensions: the momentary, and the ongoing; the mighty acts, and the silent advance. Yet they come together frequently in scripture: in promises of descendants, of land, of the Spirit, and so forth.

So the nature of blessing is that it is not a prayer belonging to one time and place. Rather, the same words of blessing are repeated over and over, in changing times and circumstances, in Israel's worship, and through the history of the Church. The words acknowledge the work of God not only in the extraordinary and extreme, but in the givens of our life and well-being.

Rather than presume that blessing comes automatically, at the end of a service we ask God to keep keeping us, as we go out seeking to reflect his face, to advance his grace, and to share his peace in the world.

Jo Bailey Wells

A refuge for you

How great are the needs of your creatures on this earth, O God. They sit there, talking quietly and quite unsuspecting, and suddenly their need erupts in all its nakedness. Then, there they are, bundles of human misery, desperate and unable to face life. And that's when my task begins.

It is not enough simply to proclaim you, God; to commend you to the hearts of others. One must also clear the path towards you in them, God, and to do that one must be a keen judge of the human soul . . . I embark on a slow voyage of exploration with everyone who comes to me.

And I thank you for the great gift of being able to read people. Sometimes they seem to me like houses with open doors. I walk in and roam through passages and rooms, and every house is furnished a little differently, and yet they are all of them the same and every one must be turned into a dwelling dedicated to you, O God.

And I promise you, yes, I promise, that I shall try to find a dwelling and a refuge for you in as many houses as possible. There are so many empty houses, and I shall prepare them all for you, the most honoured lodger. Please forgive this poor metaphor.

Etty Hillesum (1914–43), from *An Interrupted Life: The Diaries and Letters of Etty Hillesum 1941–43*

We have all heard of Anne Frank, the Jewish girl who wrote her diary in a secret attic in Amsterdam during the Nazi occupation. Not so many know of Etty Hillesum, another Jewish woman, somewhat older than Anne Frank, but still in her twenties, who was writing a diary a few streets away. Etty was a young Jewish intellectual, an intimate friend of a therapist and a student of Russian.

As the Nazis intensified their occupation of the Netherlands and anti-Jewish laws were passed, Etty found a job as a typist with the Jewish Council – the body set up to represent Jewish interests. Jews were being moved to the Westerbork transit camp outside Amsterdam, and Etty decided to go there to work. She wanted to be near her people and bring them succour.

This overwhelming prayer comes from the time when she was working here, trying to help those who were on their way to the death camps. Etty refused to leave or to hide, and in September 1943 she and her parents were placed on a transport to Auschwitz, where they perished. She threw a postcard out of the train as it left Holland, which was found by farmers. On it were written the words: 'We left the camp singing.'

During her time in Westerbork, Etty read the Old and New Testaments, as well as much else, especially her favourite poet Rainer Maria von Rilke. This prayer is full of biblical imagery – 'dwelling', 'refuge', 'open doors'. What moves me about it is its absolute compassion. Here is a young woman whose diary in its early pages shows her to be confused about life and love, taking what she can where she can. But now, a sudden and overwhelming maturity develops, and she is centred on others.

Not only that: in a strange way, it is totally incarnational. It is not enough just to speak to people about you, she tells God: I must prepare a way in them for you. And here, of course, there are echoes of Isaiah. I must, she says, see people as rooms being made ready for that most honoured lodger, who will come and dwell and remain within them. So, in one sentence, we move effortlessly from Isaiah to St John's Gospel.

How anybody could maintain this profound sense of the indwelling nature of God in the conditions of a wartime concentration camp is beyond me. It is an act of grace for which I, and countless others, are profoundly grateful.

Etty's prayer is a lesson to the contemporary Church. She shows the true way of evangelism: the way of service, of involvement, sharing the lives of others to such an extent that she becomes the herald of God's innermost presence within us, even in the face of death. Would that more of us would learn from her.

Melvyn Matthews

Anima Christi

Soul of Christ, sanctify me.
Body of Christ, save me.
Blood of Christ, inebriate me.
Water from the side of Christ, wash me.
Passion of Christ, strengthen me.
O good Jesu, hear me.
Within thy wounds, hide me.
From the malicious enemy, defend me.
In the hour of my death, call me
and bid me come to thee,
that with thy saints I may praise thee
for ever and ever.
Amen.

Anonymous

This prayer takes its name from the Latin of the opening words. But, although its use as a eucharistic devotion is familiar (popularized in the hymn 'Soul of my saviour'), its origins are uncertain.

It has often been regarded as a Jesuit prayer, associated with the Spiritual Exercises of St Ignatius Loyola, but it easily predates the Counter-Reformation, and it reflects the intense concentration on the Lord's Passion that was typical of fourteenth- and fifteenth-century devotion.

The phrase that I have always been intrigued by is 'inebriate me'. I am not alone in thinking it unusual, since it has also been rendered, 'run in my veins'. But that translation misses the point. The blood of Christ, the wine of the eucharist, is regarded as having an intoxicating effect upon souls and minds.

Perhaps there is an allusion here to Pentecost, and the bystanders' verdict on the language and behaviour of the apostles that Luke might have intended as irony: 'They are filled with new wine' (Acts 2.13). They were overpowered by the Spirit, as they became the new vessels from which the wine of the gospel was to pour forth.

Inebriation is a condition that opens up different levels of self-awareness, in which we become aware of being opaque to ourselves, freed from inhibitions, and overwhelmed, often alarmingly, by an external power. It can be a negative condition (the party and its hangover) or a positive one (Pentecost and mission). The 'Anima Christi' makes the point that positive intoxication by the new wine of the gospel and the Spirit is an integrative moment of growing in faith.

Much of my fascination with this prayer is its multifaceted presentation of ourselves in relation to Christ. Soul, body, blood, water, passion and wounds – all are terms that define who we are in our bodily, spiritual and emotional experience. This prayer uses these words to offer a devotional dissecting of the Lord's Passion that helps us to understand how we, in those same categories, function psychologically, materially and theologically as persons.

It makes me think of an article by Karl Rahner on the self-conscious knowledge of Jesus. He applies to the scriptural and doctrinal record of who Jesus is a contemporary view on how we know things. He describes knowledge as a layered dimension of human awareness, in a way that is similar to the multifaceted view of the Passion of Christ in the 'Anima Christi'.

Yet Rahner is prompting us to perceive how one can know something, but not consciously, just as you might be told of the plot of a Shakespeare play and realize that, of course, it was a story you knew well, but it had become opaque, or hidden from you.

Rahner proposes this view of knowing things as a means by which we might understand how the all-knowing, eternal Son of God lived within the limitations of human knowledge and was yet divine.

Rahner's article suggests that in the multifaceted experience of communion, to which the 'Anima Christi' directs us, we are led, through the layers of knowledge that are accessible and so 'known' to us, to a deeper capacity for God. This is a capacity that devotion renders – almost imperceptibly – less opaque, as it prepares us to know, to see, and to praise God for ever and ever.

Martin Warner

The circle of thy care

Though the dawn breaks cheerless on this Isle today,
My spirit walks upon a path of light.
For I know my greatness,
Thou hast built me a throne within thy heart.
I dwell safely within the circle of thy care.
I cannot for a moment fall out of the everlasting arms.
I am on my way to glory.

Alistair MacLean, *Hebridean Altars*

Alistair MacLean was a minister of the Church of Scotland and a Gaelic scholar. He captures a way of thinking and speaking that belonged to Hebridean people for centuries, but was disappearing with the advent of easier travel and access to radio. The First World War, then the Second, modern machinery, and the coming of television would change the lives of the people of the Hebrides in a generation or two, more than they had changed in 1,000 years. We are fortunate that Alistair MacLean collected many prayers and thoughts that were passing out of common usage.

This prayer honestly faces the reality of the cheerless isle. All days are not made up of sunshine; some are absolutely awful. I used this prayer on Holy Island on cold, damp winter mornings in church.

I also saw that 'this isle' was myself, and I had cheerless and dark days. Sometimes life feels awful. But feelings are only half the picture; they are like looking at a black-and-white photograph of flowers, and thinking that is the way they look. I say this prayer on cheerless days because of the lines that follow the first cheerless one, and so tune in to a greater reality. This is not just positive thinking: it is making oneself aware of the presence and the love of God.

Everything may appear to be against you. But an awareness of the love and protection of God can change everything. You can see the light – at least at the end of the tunnel – and you can turn towards it. Walk in a path of light. Discover your own greatness. You come from God; you belong to God; you will return to God. Even now, you are in the heart of God. Say with St Paul: 'Nothing can separate me from the love of God in Christ Jesus' (Romans 8.39). How wonderful you are to be loved by

God. Or, rather, how wonderful is the love of God to go out to you and me.

Wherever you go, whatever you do, whatever is done to you, God loves you and will never leave. You are under his care. No matter where you stray or where life takes you, he is always there. You cannot fall for a moment out of the everlasting arms. The hands that uphold us bear the nail-marks from the cross.

Our journey has an end, here described as 'glory'. When I looked up 'glory' in a theological dictionary, it gave me wonderful words such as *shekinah* and *doxa*, which relate to the hidden glory. Then it said: 'See also: God.' I didn't need to look up the reference, for I had my answer. In the words of St Augustine: 'We shall see and we shall know . . . behold our end which is no end.'

David Adam

The radiance of your face

Grant me to recognize in other men, Lord God,
the radiance of your own face.

Pierre Teilhard de Chardin (1881–1955)

The radiance of a love that so exceeds our comprehension is too much for a human being to bear. Hence the indispensability of images in our seeking to know God. Bread, wine, and water are among the images that help us to expand our vision so that we may see, through a glass darkly, the radiance of God.

But the image of God that the scriptures first draw to our attention is us – our own humanity is formed in the very image and likeness of the one who has created them.

Pierre Teilhard de Chardin was a Jesuit priest and palaeontologist who sought to redress the growing Darwinist materialism of his day by integrating theology more effectively with material science. He saw the natural world as an icon of the divine, and recognized that the tendencies of scholastic theology to associate this human *imago dei* merely with an ethereal soul had watered down its significance.

The incarnation itself proclaims to us that God's revelation in our created bodies is more than a limp and sentimental expression of a supernatural human worth. Every human body – every human face – radiates far more than this.

We are used to the manipulation of human faces as objects of pity. Images of gaunt and degraded Africans are used by anti-poverty campaigns to shock us at this unjust violation of human dignity. But Christians have to go further. For us, another human face is more than some external signpost. It is a primary site of theology, a place where we may be given a glimpse of the invisible face of God.

This is most intensely realized in the genuine face-to-face encounter – when my eyes meet another pair of eyes. No wonder, then, that our increasingly secular society is one in which face-to-face contact is in decline. The increase in virtual modes of communication, the decline in public spaces, and growing numbers of people living alone, all contribute to a society where it is easy to avoid these moments of revelation, be it in the faces of loved ones or the faces of strangers.

So a central part of 'being Church' in a way that reveals God to the world must be the face-to-face encounter with other people. This is why a 'virtual church' of atomized internet-users is a theological nonsense, as is a church confined to a particular network of like-minded people. Even in a conventional church of diverse membership, we still need to work at overcoming detachment. Have you ever exchanged the Peace with someone without making eye contact?

Churches must be places of encounter where we learn the skill for which Teilhard de Chardin prayed, so that when we go out into the world, we are able to see the face of God himself radiating from the face of the lover, the friend, and the stranger.

James Walters

More ready to hear

Almighty and everlasting God,
you are always more ready to hear than we to pray
and to give more than either we desire or deserve:
pour down upon us the abundance of your mercy,
forgiving us those things of which our conscience is afraid
and giving us those good things
which we are not worthy to ask
but through the merits and mediation
of Jesus Christ your Son our Lord,
who is alive and reigns with you,
in the unity of the Holy Spirit,
one God, now and for ever.

Collect for the 12th Sunday after Trinity, *Common Worship*

This collect has been returned in *Common Worship* to its Prayer Book date, which means it is usually read sometime in the middle of summer when many of us are away. I came to know it from the old *Alternative Service Book 1980*, where it was the collect for the Fifth Sunday in Easter.

From my days at theological college and through the early years of my ministry, the daily offices from the ASB were part of my life. Saying each collect twice a day for a week meant that many of them really sank in. This collect was one that I found I knew by heart. It is a consummate prayer. In a few short lines, we affirm the generosity of God and throw ourselves on his mercy, asking for forgiveness and blessing.

I suspect it is the honesty of the prayer I like. I am well aware that I do not make the time even I would like for prayer, let alone what God may want. Yet, the imagery in this prayer is not one of chastisement but of patient love. God is there for us, always ready to hear, always generous in giving. His mercy is abundant and we are beloved children.

When I was an ordinand, I felt I needed to work on my prayer life, and made the time to meet with a friend for half an hour of silent prayer in the chapel each week. Her Christian background was different from mine, and she seemed to sit effortlessly in prayer, while I struggled to concentrate, fretted and fidgeted. I asked her how she did it and she said to me that I was trying too hard. 'Prayer', she said, 'was like sitting down and asking God to make you a cup of tea.'

Her words have been helpful to me down the years, as I have continued to fret and fidget. They remind me that prayer is about entering into the presence of God who is always waiting to welcome me. That God longs to forgive our failings and to give us good things. Prayer is not a task of trying to make God hear us, for as soon as we begin to make the move into God's presence he is there to welcome us and make us at home.

This prayer doesn't just encourage us to pray, it also says something about how we can model ourselves on God. For we too need to be people who are ready to listen, especially to those who find it hard to have their say. We too need to be ready to forgive and generous in giving. And we can be like this because we have the knowledge of that generous, accepting, welcoming love shown to us by God himself – God who is always more ready to hear than we are to pray, yet who through Jesus will give us far more than we desire or deserve.

Emma Percy

Life's treasure

At the beginning of time and at the end
you are God and I bless you.
At my birth and in my dying,
in the opening of the day and at its close,
in my waking and my sleeping,
you are God and I bless you.
You are the first and the last,
the giver of every gift,
the presence without whom there would be no present,
the life without whom there is no life.
Lead me to the heart of life's treasure
that I may be a bearer of the gift.
Lead me to the heart of the present
that I may be a sharer of your eternal presence.

J. Philip Newell, from *Sounds of the Eternal*

━━━◗◐◈◉◈◐◗◈❋◈◗◐◈◉◈◐◗━━━

Thich Nhat Hanh, the Vietnamese Buddhist teacher and Nobel Peace Prize nominee, began a talk in Edinburgh by saying: 'We all have an appointment with life, and the time of the appointment is now.'

All the great traditions of spirituality, whether from East or West, teach the importance of presence, of being alive to the gift of the moment, and attentive to the presence of God at the heart of each moment. It is a simple teaching, but not an easy practice.

At the most important moments of life, of course, we practise presence quite naturally. At the birth of our children, in the discovery of love, at the death of our parents, in situations of sudden danger, we are alive to the moment. We experience the wonder and pleasure, or the pain and fear, of what is happening.

But most of the time we live at a type of distance from the present. We get imprisoned by the past or bound by the future. The details of yesterday distract us; the worries of tomorrow preoccupy us; and we end up missing the moment. This prayer is an attempt to call us back to the present. God is now, always now, and it is now that we are invited to be people of presence, alive to the Presence without whom there would be no present.

A few years ago I met a Jewish man in New Jersey who had become, of all things, a Presbyterian minister. We spoke about important moments, and he told me about a boyhood experience that had shaped his life. He was at a summer camp for Jewish boys just outside New York. Word got round that the Rebbe, the much loved rabbi of their Hasidic community, was downstream from the camp and was prepared to spend time with the boys.

They rushed along the riverbank and found the Rebbe standing in the middle of the stream, rocking back and forth in prayer. He was practising what the Jewish mystics call 'one-pointed concentration', looking for the presence of God at the heart of the moment.

The Rebbe said only one thing to the boys. 'The water that we see flowing past us now will never flow past us again.' He then returned to his rhythmic movement of prayer, and the boys joined him in the river. The combination of physically rocking back and forth, plus the steady flow of the stream, sent the boy to sleep.

When he woke up, all the other boys had gone, and he was standing alone, held by the Rebbe, who was continuing to rock in prayer. The Rebbe didn't say anything, but he looked into the boy's face and smiled. His countenance was like an icon. It was a lens through which the young boy glimpsed something of the Presence.

With some bewilderment, I asked my Jewish friend why he, when he had received such a gift in his own religious tradition, had become a Christian. He said: 'Because I found in Christ what that Rebbe taught me to see. I found in Christ the one who is present.'

Early in the Christian tradition, Jesus is referred to as 'Emmanuel', 'God with us' (Matthew 1.23). He is experienced as carrying the presence of God, not simply in the glory of his birth and the glow of transfiguration light, but in the rejection and ignominy of the cross. He recalls us to what we have forgotten. He is the memory of what is first or deepest in us and in every situation: the presence of God.

'Lead me to the heart of the present, O God, that I may be a sharer of your eternal presence.'

J. Philip Newell

Creation

Born anew

As earth requires rest
and the seas need time to be replenished,
so in resting may I be made more alive,
so in stillness may my creativity be born anew.
Bless me in the night, O God,
that I may wake refreshed.
With your ministering messengers of sleep
bless me in the night.

J. Philip Newell, from *Sounds of the Eternal*

⸺◦❖◦❖◦❖◦❖◦ ❋ ◦❖◦❖◦❖◦❖◦⸺

There is a relationship between stillness and creativity; between resting and being more alive. There is a pattern woven through all creation: of night followed by day; of the stillness of the winter earth followed by the energy of spring; of long periods of infolding followed by colourful unfoldings; of life's seed-force slowly regenerating in the dark before bursting forth for conception and new beginnings.

Are we thinking that we can ignore this pattern and still be creative? Are we thinking that we can be constantly busy, or that we can relentlessly push our own resources and the resources of the earth, and still enjoy well-being in our lives and relationships?

Whether physically or spiritually, if we ignore nature's patterns of stillness, our creativity will be either superficial or exhausted. This prayer points to the sacredness of rest. It names our need for inner restfulness, as well as outer restfulness, if we are to be deeply alive.

A centuries-old story from the Western Isles of Scotland tells of Mary the Mother taking a journey with the Christ-child across one of the Hebridean islands. She grows weary, but on the path meets a milking-maid who is rushing off to work. Mary asks the young woman to hold the child so that she can rest awhile, to which the maid replies: 'I can't possibly stop. I have six cows to milk.' The maid then hurries on her way to get the day's work done.

Further along the path, Mary meets a second milking-maid, who has

12 cows to milk. The second maid, however, agrees to pause and hold the child. She plays with him and suckles him while Mary rests. The story concludes by saying that, although the second maid had twice as many cows as the first, she finished her day's work in half the time and with four times as much milk.

It doesn't always work out that way, of course; but we know what the story is saying. We know in our lives that when we have neglected creation's rhythm of day and night, of times of striving counterbalanced by times of being and playfulness, or when we have thought that we somehow are above nature's cycles, our refusal to be still or to let go becomes counterproductive. Our frenetic pace cuts us off from the deep creative energies that are within us, made as we are in the image of the creator.

The ninth-century Irish teacher Eriugena taught that both nature and grace flow from God. They both are sacred. Both are expressions of God's goodness. Nature, he said, is the gift of being, and grace is the gift of well-being.

Grace is given, not that we may become other than natural, but that we may become truly natural. It is given, not that we may become more than creation, but that we may know ourselves to be part of creation. The graces of renewal that can come to us in resting from work, or in the silence of the night, or in the calm of meditative prayer and stillness, are given to free us from the unnaturalness of what we have become. They are given to release in us again the renewing streams of health and creativity that God has placed at the core of our being.

'As earth requires rest and the seas need time to be replenished, so in resting may I be made more alive, so in stillness may my creativity be born anew.'

J. Philip Newell

The glory of the everlasting world

That your glory rises in the morning sun
and sparkles off flowing waters;
that the glory of the everlasting world
shines in this world,
growing from the ground
and issuing forth in every creature;
that glory can be handled, seen and known
in the matter of earth and human relationships
and the most ordinary matters of daily life,
assure me again this day, O God,
assure me again this day.

J. Philip Newell, from *Sounds of the Eternal*

The prophecy of Isaiah says that 'the whole earth is full of God's glory' (Isaiah 6.3). Ecclesiasticus's way of putting it is that creation is 'sparkling' with God's light (Ecclesiasticus 42.22). Similarly, St Paul says 'there is a glory of the sun and a glory of the moon and a glory of the stars' (1 Corinthians 15.41).

There is a shining of God's presence deep within all that has been created. It is like a subterranean river, running through all things. If somehow that flow were to be dammed up, creation would cease to exist. Glory is not simply a characteristic of certain moments and certain places; it belongs to the essence of life's stream, for every person and every creature comes forth from that brilliance.

Genesis 1, with its 'let there be light', is pointing to the light that is at the heart of life. In that sense, it is the beginning of all things. Our genesis is in God. How are our eyes to be opened to this deep glory? How do we learn to see it in dark and confusing times, as well as in the dull and grey moments of life? This prayer is an attempt to seek an assurance of the glory that is always present, but often hidden.

We have glimpsed glory in our lives at particular times more than at others – in the awareness of morning light dawning over a sleeping city; in the glistening of freshly washed fruit beside a kitchen sink; in the compassion of tears shining in another's eyes. Similarly, we have been better at naming it at certain points, historically, than at others. There were medieval philosophers who wanted to say that *theos*, Greek for 'God', was derived from the verb *theo*, 'to flow' or 'to run', for God is the one who flows through all things. Kenneth White, the Scottish poet, calls this 'the glow flow'. It is the light that glistens from within life.

This is not to confuse creation with the eternal glory. It is, however, to say that it is in and through creation that we glimpse the glory. The Jewish mystics make a fine distinction when they describe the lights of creation as the adornments of God. It is like a man loving a woman who is beautifully clothed. He will be aware of her splendid garments, for they carry her scent and express her vivacity, but the focus of his desire is the woman, not her clothing. In the Hasidic tradition, this is referred to as a yearning to see 'the great shining of the world's inwardness'.

One of the favourite sayings of Lord Macleod of Fuinary, the founder of the modern-day Iona Community in Scotland, was 'matter matters'. At the heart of the material is the spiritual. Deep within this world is the glory of the everlasting world. What we do to creation, therefore, what we do to our own and one another's bodies, what we do with the earth's resources, is a spiritual issue. To pray for our seeing to be cleansed is to pray for our handling of matter to be transformed.

'That glory can be handled, seen and known in the matter of earth and human relationships and in the most ordinary matters of daily life, assure me again this day, O God, assure me again this day.'

J. Philip Newell

Life-giving rays

I bind unto myself today
The virtues of the starlit heaven,
The glorious sun's life-giving ray,
The whiteness of the moon at even,
The flashing of the lightning free,
The whirling wind's tempestuous shocks,
The stable earth, the deep salt sea,
Around the old eternal rocks.
I bind unto myself today
The power of God to hold and lead,
His eye to watch, his might to stay,
His ear to hearken to my need.
The wisdom of my God to teach,
His hand to guide, his shield to ward;
The word of God to give me speech,
His heavenly host to be my guard.

St Patrick's Breastplate (ascribed to St Patrick, 372–466,
translated by Mrs C. F. Alexander)

The original text of *St Patrick's Breastplate* says simply:

I arise today
With the powers of heaven,
The sun in brightness,
The moon in splendour,
The flashing of fire,
The swift stroke of lightning . . .

These powers of nature are my companions. They were around long before me, and will be there long after me. From my limited point of view, they may sometimes be terrifying and destructive. But they and I are part of the same creative process.

We are in one family together. So I can know them, as St Francis did, as Brother Sun, Sister Moon, and even as Sister Death. They are created as things that are good in themselves; they are not merely things for me to exploit or play with. Still less are they commodities for me to claim a corner in, to own, in competition with other people.

When I start the day with this prayer, I am committing myself to the Creator. I will look around and sing: 'The earth is the Lord's and all that is in it: The world and its people belong to the Lord' (Psalm 24.1).

With eyes open to this commitment, I will look at my house, my street, my work, my wealth, the products that I use. Above all, I will look at the land, the 'stable earth'. This is one thing that humans did not make and cannot make. Yet we deal with it as if it were just another commodity, to be divided up and claimed, in competition with each other. I will recognize that the earth and the wealth that comes from it are all on loan to us, to the whole human race, and not merely to those who have managed to grasp the levers of control.

This is one of the verses of the *Breastplate* that are 'starred' in older hymnbooks – to be treated as optional – and are totally omitted in newer ones. I think that St Patrick and Mrs Alexander, as people of Celtic lands, would be dismayed. If we don't get our commitment to the Creator right, we shall have nothing for the sacraments of redemption to claim and work on.

From the Creation, my eye and my commitment are led to the Creator. At the heart of the universe there is not just an impersonal force nor even a designing mind. There is one who is eye and ear and hand and speech.

Comparatively speaking, I am blind, deaf, crippled, dumb, and have great learning difficulties. The differences between me and those who carry the official label 'disabled' are insignificant. In belonging to society and Church, I am just a member of a patients' co-operative. If any is excluded, I am excluded, too. But God is on our side. God enables us in our dis-ability. God claims us with such abilities as we have, to use in co-operation with the abilities of our fellow pilgrims.

As I move into the day, I do so in company with Christ, who was blindfolded, who was not listened to, who was pinned down immobile, who was reckoned to be stupid or crazy, and who now carries the scars caused by those who treated him as expendable. As Dietrich Bonhoeffer said: 'Christ has come as our Brother, and wants no honour for himself as long as his sisters or brothers are dishonoured.'

I move into this day with this kind of status to empower me, this kind of vision to inspire me, this kind of awareness to hear me, this kind of companionship to protect me.

John D. Davies

Lay me down

Lord, lay me down like a stone, and raise me up like fresh bread.

Leo Tolstoy, *War and Peace*, Book XII, chapter 13

Good things come in small packets. These 14 words are the nightly prayer of Platon Karataev, a Russian peasant soldier in Tolstoy's *War and Peace*. In this novel with a cast of thousands, Karataev is the archetypal peasant. Pierre, his fellow prisoner of war, is overwhelmed by Karataev's simplicity, courage and ability to cope with hardship, danger and loss. Karataev is indomitable.

Every night since infancy, from Karataev's heart has come this very simple prayer. Deep faith and wisdom are gathered in a tiny working space.

Prayer enables us to see things as God sees them. Mother Julian saw the world as a nut in the palm of her hand. The well-heeled characteristically do things to death by analysing them or attempting to manage them. The powerless peasant can do neither, and knows better. He accepts the underlying unity of everything in God – the cycles of rest and work, night and day, death and life. Karataev fashions prayer out of daily reality. He pictures two peasant occupations: laying down stones and baking bread.

In scripture, God is the rock, whose stability, reflected by Mount Zion, undergirds his people. Laying down stones for a pillow at Bethel, Jacob saw heaven opened, and angels ascending and descending on a ladder (Genesis 28.10–17). In Christ, God has laid down for his people a rock that cannot be removed. The stone the builders rejected has become the head of the corner.

Bread is the staff of life. God's mercy for his people in the wilderness comes in the form of manna: bread they did not know, the bread of angels. Manna was renewed every morning, and confounded all attempts to store it. If you've ever tried stale baguette, you'll know how soon fresh bread becomes uneatable.

Jesus taught his followers to pray for their daily bread, and offered himself to the world as the bread of life. Karataev's prayer makes the process of bread rising a great symbol of all human living. Jesus taught that 'the Kingdom of heaven is like leaven which a woman took and hid in three measures of meal, till it was all leavened' (Matthew 13.33).

How, in a passing world, can we set our hearts on a world that will never end? The unwise, supposing they can manage change, are often nostalgic about their imagined past, setting tradition against renewal. Peasants must accept whatever life brings, and cope. The peasant Karataev knows that everything is in God's hands. God gives stability and decay and new life. He is the only context of everything that happens.

Karataev's prayer expresses what it truly is to be created: not finished products, turned out on a factory line, but persons, constantly, dynamically being made and remade by God. Understanding and accepting this fact produces the strength to cope with any test.

God creatively touches and transforms all our lives from within. Today and tomorrow and the day after, new every morning until the world's last day, he is renewed within us who renews us. Arise, sleeper, and awake from the dead, and Christ shall give you light!

Alan Wilson

Joy

The royalty of inward happiness

Grant to us, O Lord, the royalty of inward happiness, and the serenity which comes from living close to thee. Daily renew in us the sense of joy, and let the eternal spirit of the Father dwell in our souls and bodies, filling every corner of our hearts with light and grace; so that, bearing about with us the infection of good courage, we may be diffusers of life, and may meet all ills and cross accidents with gallant and high-hearted happiness, giving thee thanks always for all things.

Robert Louis Stevenson (1850–94)

This prayer has the most wonderful phrases. The 'royalty of inward happiness' is amazing: a 'royalty' is a sort of unearned reward, and 'inward happiness', when it comes, does give you a sense of being graced; being given something you did not work for nor deserve. It fills you with dignity and life.

Further on, 'bearing about with us the infection of good courage', is so right because 'good courage' is something that we can pass to others just by being near them. The word 'infection' saves us from being self-righteous and telling people to be joyful all the time.

I love it when I get to that phrase 'meet all ills and cross accidents with gallant and high-hearted happiness'. 'Cross accidents' are those that cross our path and give us the cross to bear (as well as make us cross). Meanwhile, 'gallant', so little used nowadays, is such a great word to use about happiness: it conveys the gallantry that happiness enables in us. It also reminds me of the top sails of a square-rigged ship, one of which is called the 'topgallant', and which carries the ship along with style and speed.

This is a prayer in which the language illustrates the meaning, and fills you with the life it is talking about as you read or speak it. It is also about joy. Joy seems to be in such short supply and such a hard-won virtue. The prayer contradicts that. It says that you can be carried about by joy in everyday life. This is not the way we usually see things. We think of joy as having to be achieved in some way, or at least we think that joy is not our normal condition.

Robert Louis Stevenson is clear that joy is readily available, and given to us. It fills us with light, so that we can 'infect' everything we do and everybody we meet with the same joy. The prayer implies that joy is there, but we have forgotten about it somehow – lost it by our preoccupation with overcoming things ourselves. Joy is ready for us, and we have to open ourselves to it and let it fill our lives.

But there's another thing the prayer is saying. It recognizes that our lives are random and chancey. All sorts of things can and do happen, many of them unwelcome. But the point is that joy is not something we then have to summon up to counteract these 'cross accidents': instead, joy is part of what is happening to us, essentially part of what we are given in everyday life.

We can be joyful almost because everything is chancy and full of play. Treating whatever comes not as an obstacle, but as a gift, is joy. Life is not against us, this prayer says, but all life – all creation, our whole existence – is full of the joy we think we have to obtain somewhere else.

Melvyn Matthews

Rejoice in comradeship

Strengthen, we beseech Thee, O Lord, the wills of Thy faithful servants;
that they, ardently withstanding the Empires of this world,
may rejoice in the comradeship of Thy Kingdom:
through Jesus Christ, Thy Son, our Lord,
Who liveth and reigneth with Thee,
in the unity of the Holy Ghost, ever one God,
world without end. Amen.

Conrad Noel (1869–1942), 'The Crusader's Prayer',
from the devotions of the Catholic Crusade

Rather like its author, this prayer was never going to be accepted within the mainstream of the Church of England. The Revd Conrad Noel was one of the more extreme and colourful of the socialist-minded Anglo-Catholic clergy of the early twentieth century.

Known as the 'Red Vicar' of Thaxted in Essex, Noel viewed socialism as the inevitable outworking of the gospel, and he rooted his radical social teaching in the writings of the Early Fathers. His controversial ministry reached its climax when he replaced the Union flag in the nave of his church with the Red Flag and the flags of St George and Sinn Fein. Riots broke out in the village, and high-minded undergraduates from Cambridge drove down to join in the 'battle of the flags'.

But what merits our attention in this prayer is Noel's utter confidence that positive social change is to be found nowhere apart from the gospel. The prayer was written for the members of the Catholic Crusade, a movement that Noel founded in 1918, in response to his frustration with the pragmatism and gradualism of other left-wing church groups.

Noel rooted these failures in the lack of definite theological foundations. Only the 'full Catholic Faith' could bring about real revolution, and so the Crusade was formed 'to encourage the rising of the people in the might of the Risen Christ and the Saints, mingling Heaven and earth that we may shatter this greedy world to bits'.

To us today, Noel's life and teaching has a quaint feel to it, rather like hearing the stories of an eccentric great-uncle. We may smile at how anachronistic the Marxist language of empire and comradeship sounds in our post-Cold War era, not to mention how incongruous in the language of prayer.

Yet perhaps this is more a poor reflection on the insipidness of our own political culture and language of prayer. Noel lived in a time of great political upheaval, when oppressive empires really were being overthrown by men and women who wanted a fairer share of wealth and opportunity. Too often, the Church was caught up in the conservatism of empire – not least the C of E, which Noel branded 'not a religion but a disease'. Noel recognized that true Christianity could not collude in this way: the kingdom of God was about tangible mutuality (comradeship) with others, and not the perpetuation of worldly hierarchies.

So this prayer challenges us to consider carefully what kind of kingdom we are praying for. Do our prayers reflect the view of Christianity (which Marx held and Noel opposed) as the spiritual endorsement of the status quo, with a little pietistic tinkering around the edges?

The British Empire against which Noel prayed and preached may be dead. But, if imperialism is about the imposition of systems of control on the weak by the strong, then, as long as leaders of the most powerful nations continue to make decisions that affect the whole world, we might think about how modern-day empires still need to be withstood. If the kingdom of God really does require us to make poverty history, then perhaps we need some of Conrad Noel's rhetoric in our prayers today, too.

James Walters

Lightness of being

Lord Christ,
help us to have the courage and humility to name our burdens
and lay them down
so that we are light to walk across the water
to where you beckon us.

Our pride,
armouring us,
hardening us,
making us defend our dignity by belittling others.

We name it and we lay it down.

The memory of hurts and insults,
driving us to lash out,
to strike back.

We name it and we lay it down.

Our antagonism against those
whose actions, differences, presence,
threaten our comfort or security.

We name it and we lay it down.

Our fear,
of unsolved questions,
of the unknown,
of fear itself.

We name it and we lay it down.

We do not need these burdens,
but we have grown used to carrying them,
have forgotten what it is like to be light.
Beckon us to lightness of being,
for you show us it is not unbearable.
Only so can we close the distance.
Only so can we walk upon the water.

Blessed are you, Lord Christ, who make heavy burdens light.

Kathy Galloway (b. 1952), from *Talking to the Bones*

Do you remember the novel *The Unbearable Lightness of Being* by the Czech writer, Milan Kundera? Kundera was somebody who wanted to challenge the heavy hand of communism in his country by a mixture of laughter, mockery and fantasy. He thought this would work better than serious political opposition, which made communism more important than it was.

This approach to communism reminds me of one of my teachers at theological college, who used to say that John the Baptist came into the world dressed in skins, like any good prophet, saying 'Repent!'; while Jesus came turning cartwheels and saying something like: 'Come off it.' He could have added: 'Don't take yourself so seriously.'

This is a prayer that Christians should not take themselves and their burdens so seriously. Jesus' criticism of the Pharisees was just that: 'Lighten up,' he might have said in modern English.

Like the Pharisees, we are in danger of making our act of repentance so important that grace doesn't have a chance of reaching us because of all our heavy repenting. People do become obsessed with their own sin, and talk endlessly about their problems. They are never free of them because they are always talking about how they might be free. This is an obsessional self-preoccupation that only a good dose of ridicule or laughter can cure (although some are so ill that laughter fails to work).

Grace is a form of lightness of being that refuses to take itself seriously – indeed, refuses to consider 'self' at all because to do so means that self gets in the way. This is perhaps what some of the mystics were talking about, and I was glad to have this confirmed by Denys Turner, the Norris-Hulse Professor of Theology at Cambridge, a student of mysticism. He makes the point that the mystics were not so much concerned with finding a way to God through experiences of personal union, but with criticizing the way in which preoccupation with spiritual experiences prevented people from allowing God to exercise his total freedom in them. He develops this idea in his book *The Darkness of God* (Cambridge University Press, 1995).

Looked at in this way, mysticism is not for the few, but for all of us, because it is a sort of lightness of being, a total freedom, where we stop thinking about the importance of having a mystical experience at all. That might be unbearable, which is why so many of us in the Church reject mysticism today.

Melvyn Matthews

Victory is ours

Goodness is stronger than evil;
Love is stronger than hate;
Light is stronger than darkness;
Life is stronger than death;
Victory is ours through him who loves us.

Desmond Tutu, from *An African Prayer Book*

In the dark church, whether at the Advent carol service or early on Easter morning, I am struck by how much light comes from a single candle. 'It is better to light one candle than sit in the darkness for ever' – but the Christian hope is for much more. St John voiced the hope that, in Christ, 'the light shines in the darkness and the darkness did not overcome it' (John 1.5). The light has already won the battle with darkness: 'Victory is ours through him who loves us.'

It was a huge shock to me, aged 18, to encounter the realities of apartheid in, of all places, Durham University. A fellow student was a South African political exile, and his mail had always been opened before he got it. I have no idea what the South African secret service thought it was doing, but I wasn't the only one to respond by joining the Anti-Apartheid Movement.

At King's College, London, my links with South Africans were strengthened. King's trained a number of black clergy who would be leaders against apartheid, and be well prepared to hold positions of great responsibility when it ended, such as Archbishop Desmond Tutu.

St Martin-in-the-Fields is next door to the South African High Commission. On the eve of the 1998 Lambeth Conference, we held a service for the Church of the Province of Southern Africa and its British diocesan associations. Afterwards, the High Commissioner invited us to a reception. Few of the South African bishops had been inside before, and their eyes opened wide in delighted disbelief.

In the face of oppression, Archbishop Desmond Tutu had the confidence to laugh. He knew that the victory was already won. This prayer is one of the great prayers of an oppressed people. A government fell, as Archbishop Tutu knew it eventually would.

'Victory is ours' is one of the best in a fine collection of prayers in Archbishop Tutu's *An African Prayer Book*. There are ancient prayers from

Augustine and North Africa. There is Archbishop Trevor Huddleston's 'God bless Africa', which countless people prayed after reading *Naught for your Comfort*. There is a wonderfully evocative African canticle:

> All you big things, bless the Lord.
> Mount Kilimanjaro and Lake Victoria,
> The Rift Valley and the Serengeti Plain,
> Fat baobabs and shady mango trees,
> All eucalyptus and tamarind trees,
> Bless the Lord.
> Praise and extol him for ever.

After the 1998 Lambeth Conference, as we tried to understand the painful divisions among Anglicans, the late Bishop John V. Taylor preached at St Martin's, and spoke about the importance of creation for Africans. He also contrasted the European's 'I think; therefore I am' with the African feeling that 'I belong; therefore I am.'

In our small world, with our big differences of experience and perception, one of the most pressing questions for us is how we belong to each other. South Africa has taught the world to celebrate our God-given diversity. Saying this prayer, you can hear the infectious joyous laughter of one who is utterly confident that God will see us through a crisis, and take us to a deeper truth and greater reality.

Nicholas Holtam

Faith

A present of myself

Lord, I make you a present of myself. I do not know what to do with myself. So let me make this exchange: I will place myself entirely in your hands, if you will cover my ugliness with your beauty, and tame my unruliness with your love. Put out the flames of false passion in my heart, since these flames destroy all that is true within me. Make me always busy in your service.

Lord, I want no special signs from you, nor am I looking for intense emotions in response to your love. I would rather be free of all emotion than run the danger of falling victim once again to false passion. Let my love for you be naked, without any emotional clothing.

Catherine of Genoa (1447–1510)

Despite a pious childhood and a desire to enter religious life, Catherine of Genoa was nevertheless obedient to her brothers' wishes. Her father had died, leaving the family's finances in a fragile state. Regarding her as a valuable asset, her brothers formed a much-needed dynastic alliance by marrying her at 16 to the even younger Giuliano Adorno.

The marriage was loveless, violent, faithless and abusive. Catherine suffered depression, emptiness and loneliness. Without much success, she sought her escape in superficial pleasure. Years later, while kneeling in confession, she felt herself pierced through by the divine light, and fell into a rapture of ecstasy. And so she began a series of mystical experiences.

Although so enclosed within herself that she was unable to share her visions with anyone else until not long before her death, she gave herself over to good works for the poor. In time, her self-evident holiness won over even her husband to a reformed life.

Her complex prayer may perhaps be overdone, but many aspects of her life find themselves entrenched in it. The prayer speaks of her sense of unworthiness before God: her 'ugliness' and 'unruliness'. She speaks of giving herself entirely over into God's hands, and asks to be kept busy. She wants nothing more than to be lost in God to escape her own life.

One can see the marks of her own psychological wounds beneath the pious device of juxtaposing human wretchedness and divine glory. Her long inability to share her visions with others hints at her struggle to articulate her true self.

Yet this is also the wonderful pivotal point when Catherine's prayer races away from her abusive past. She engages teasingly with God. She 'wants no special signs', though we know, as she surely knows, that God has privileged her with ecstatic visions. She simply wants to love God, 'free of all emotion'; yet her spiritual love-dance with God is more than most of us can imagine.

It is rather Anglican to feel uncomfortable with emotion. How often do we still hear how challenging the offering of the Peace is for our congregations? The extension of a handshake is often stiff and self-conscious, yet one step too far for many.

Although intensely personal, Catherine's love for God is not free of emotion; her love for God has not much to do with Anglican politeness, but is drenched in passion. It is not intellectual, nor perhaps entirely pure. It may be that it veers towards the sexually subliminal. It doesn't matter. What matters is that Catherine is naked before God, and that God's love for us can legitimately enflame a love that engulfs us.

What also matters is the recognition that our authentic prayer is never decoupled from who we are and from what we have experienced. There are some who may deny the traces of self-loathing in Catherine's prayer, or the intimations of emotional escapism in her love for God. For me, they are the very reasons why her prayer is so powerful. It is a self-offering. Her love of God does not remove her scars; for her scars are surely one with her. She doesn't escape herself, but, just as she is, she offers herself up to God.

Many of us can identify with Catherine. Our lives are not as we would have wished them to be. Disappointments and pain have left their mark. We, too, may find it hard to share our inner life or to open our hearts. But we, too, can be certain that, no matter our ugliness or our sadness, our Saviour is waiting to be our partner in a never-ending dance of love.

Mark Speeks

Into your hands

Into your hands, Lord, we commit our spirit,
into your hands, the open and defenceless hands of love,
into your hands, the accepting and welcoming hands of love,
into your hands, the firm and reliable hands of love,
we commit our spirit.

Rex Chapman (b. 1938), Canon of Carlisle Cathedral,
from *The Glory of God*

I associate this prayer with some pottery hands I got from the island of Patmos some years ago. Those hands are important to me. Whenever I take them away to use at a quiet day or a parish conference I flinch inwardly – what if they get broken?

They've taken on this almost sacramental significance because I've placed myself in them so often. Hopeful, wounded, expectant, exhausted – I've placed myself in God's hands, symbolized by these clay copies, and let myself be sustained or encouraged or restored by the gentle embrace of God.

Above all, perhaps, I've simply rested there. 'Into your hands, Lord, I commit my spirit.' Learning to rest in the hands of God is one of the most important breakthroughs in many a journey of prayer. Stilling the agitated mind and simply being present to the presence of God is often a hard-won discipline, but it is like water in the desert for an overworked priest or a harassed commuter.

That same resting is also one of our most urgent tasks in a Church distracted by many issues and false idols. We're easily seduced into thinking that every problem needs to be resolved as quickly as possible, whereas often problems need to be held in the 'open and defenceless hands of love', while the Spirit resolves our pain at a deeper level and over a much longer period.

My pottery hands are at times not only God's hands for me, but also my hands, open to God. Here is my life offered up to God, and I need to make that offering without strings. Closed hands might conceal much; open hands reveal all to the One I choose to trust. As he takes my life,

I'm both relieved and, if I'm honest, a bit anxious about offering so much with so little control. But that's faith; that's the deal.

This prayer by Rex Chapman sinks itself deeply into the Passion of Jesus. There's nothing weak and resigned about these words from the cross, and nothing anxious either. Luke tells us Jesus said these words with a loud voice, summoning all his energy to hurl himself into his Father's arms. We, too, commit our spirit to the 'firm and reliable hands of love'.

This is a prayer for the start of the day, when we go off to live the detail of discipleship in what often feels like a foreign land; and also for the end of the day, when everything is returned to the gentle place of rest – the Father's love. My pottery hands are a powerful symbol for me in my place of prayer. If they did get broken, I suppose I'd just have to return to Patmos for a while.

John Pritchard

Our trust in you

Like your disciples on the road to Emmaus,
we are so often incapable of seeing that you, O Christ,
are our companion on the way.
But, when our eyes are opened, we realize that you were speaking to us,
even though perhaps we had forgotten you.
Then the sign of our trust in you is that, in our turn,
we try to love, to forgive with you.
Independent of our doubts or even our faith,
O Christ, you are always there:
your love burns in our heart of hearts.

Brother Roger Schutz (1915–2005),
Prior of the Taizé Community

I first went to Taizé in the 1960s with a group of young English people. French Protestants found the place amazing. Our hosts said: 'You Anglicans will love this. They kneel down to pray!' And in those days they did. Since then, they have removed almost all the furniture from the great church and use prayer stools. Most of the (largely young) congregation sit on the floor to pray.

We heard the remarkable story of the genesis of the community and the faithfulness of Brother Roger and his companions to the life of prayer and the ministry of reconciliation and unity.

Over the years, I returned to make a number of retreats there. One was in a small tent in the silent field adjoining the community church, where I spent a week reading a book about the Beatitudes. I remember it as a turning point in my ministry.

This prayer by Brother Roger, the Prior of Taizé, speaks of what I first found in that community and what is still fresh now. As a result of those visits, I became convinced that God was not so much far away, waiting for me to come to him, but very close by, within me somehow, and perhaps 'nearer than breathing, closer than hands and feet'.

I became aware that I was in danger of striving for salvation when salvation was being offered to me, from within my own being, by the Christ who was there waiting for me to discover him. I came to a sense of the presence of Christ deep in my existence – a presence that I had forgotten about, or perhaps found difficulty in believing was there, but which was actually sustaining me all the while and was hidden in all things.

Yet this prayer and those retreats also speak to me of how, because of our awareness of the presence of Christ in our lives, we can turn, and, with Christ in us, love others and be reconciled to them, because this is a possibility for us in our life with Christ. It is he who lives this life within us. Our task is to release that life from the depths of our being. The work of prayer and reconciliation is not so much mine to achieve as Christ's within me, which I must allow a full place in my life.

This prayer – and the life of the Taizé community behind it – reminds us that prayer that does not lead to a reconciled life is one where there is no 'sign of our trust'. If we do not recognize that Christ is at work, independent of our doubts 'or even our faith', then what we are saying is that our life is all our own, and that we can see it all and know what it is about.

We admit, by our lack of reconciliation, not only that we do not trust, but also that we think we can see everything that is at work in our lives. There is no mystery, no grace, nothing else than what we know about and can control. Somehow, we cannot admit that Christ has occupied our hearts before we knew about him.

The good news about our lives is that Christ goes on working in us, independently of what we know or do, or even believe. That is a real cause for joy. The question is whether we can believe it.

Melvyn Matthews

The riches of your grace

Almighty God,
in Christ you make all things new:
transform the poverty of our nature by the
**   riches of your grace,**
and in the renewal of our lives
make known your heavenly glory;
through Jesus Christ our Lord.
Amen.

Collect for the 2nd Sunday of Epiphany,
Common Worship

Epiphany is a time of wonder, a time of imagining a new community. The veil between heaven and earth is rolled back and the glistening glory of God is revealed – to the Magi in Bethlehem, to John and those gathered for baptism at the Jordan, to the disciples and revellers at the wedding in Cana.

The second and third lines of the prayer have a rhythmic lilt, with the stress on every third or fourth syllable: poverty, riches, grace, renewal, lives. The logic would be to move up from poverty to riches, and then down from renewal to some suitable earthly disappointment. But, instead, the contrast between human poverty and divine riches is followed by the harmony of renewed lives and heavenly glory. Thus the prayer takes the believer through salvation history, from Israel in exile ('poverty'), to Jesus ('grace'), to the Church (renewed 'lives'), and finally to the end of time ('heavenly glory').

'The poverty of our nature': ten years as a priest in areas of social deprivation gave me time to ponder the contours of poverty. It took me a long time to learn that poverty isn't really about money. Poverty, I now believe, is about not knowing what to do, or knowing what to do but having no one with whom to do it. In other words, poverty is about imagination and community.

If you have imagination, if you have been given and have received permission to use your creativity, to perceive needs and to develop skills; and if you have a community – a supportive family, or a network of people committed to working to a more or less coherent goal – then, even if you are short of money, you are not genuinely poor; and if you gain access to money, you will probably use it wisely. But if you lack either the imagination or the community, if you have never had the courage or encouragement to dream, or if you have never had the opportunity or perseverance to maintain relationships of trust, money probably won't help you much.

If poverty is about imagination and community, so is sin. Life as a pastor has taught me that most sin – my own, just as much as others' – is a failure to wonder or a failure to trust. In this sense, we are all poor: poor in imagination (wonder), or poor in community (trust). But this prayer is a prayer for transformation. Not for the eradication of our nature, but for us to spring up like a jack-in-the-box once the lid of our sin is removed. As Thomas Aquinas promised, grace does not destroy nature, but perfects it.

And here is the astonishing request: that God's glory may be revealed, not in spite of our shortcomings, but through their transformation. The glory of God is made visible in our becoming fully alive. In renewed lives (which we can't attain, but can only receive), we discover a new community: a new possibility of trust. In heavenly glory, we have plenty to stretch our imaginations: an eternity of wonder.

Sam Wells

Trust in the Lord

Blessed are those who trust in the Lord,
    whose trust is the Lord.
They shall be like a tree planted by water,
    sending out its roots by the stream.
It shall not fear when heat comes,
    and its leaves shall stay green;
in the year of drought it is not anxious,
    and it does not cease to bear fruit.

Jeremiah 17.7–8 (NRSV)

I have often found that scripture reads better when it is absorbed at the deepest level of one's inner consciousness; so this short passage from Jeremiah is a prayer in itself. It is the kind of prayer that allows a person simply to rest, or be still, in God.

It can be read at times when words fail us. I find it best to read it from within that place of stillness which is created by choosing to make space for God in the haste and noise of daily living, or at the end of a long day.

It can be helpful to recall some of the desert fathers when praying like this. St Anthony of Egypt, for example, is best remembered for the great agony of mind that he endured in the desert. His desert, like ours, was likely to have been a desolation of mind and spirit, not simply a matter of physical privation, since he is renowned for having battled with temptations. There is no greater loneliness than battling with temptations, no matter how trivial or mundane these may seem to be. He was also called to a life of poverty; and this, in a sense, is also a calling we all share.

Poverty is not an end in itself, but the means to true freedom and to the spiritual wealth that is to be gained in Christian discipleship. Far too many people are not in the privileged position of choosing whether or not to embrace poverty, of course, but have it thrust upon them, often as a result of the western world's relentless pursuit of material things. Yet there is a sense in which poverty that is freely chosen can still be considered a virtue.

As the prayer suggests, trusting in God implies a spiritual poverty. This is a desire and need for God that frees people from the distractions of more 'instant' material wants. When the gifts that the world has to bestow are seen for what they are, with the limited benefits they confer, they no longer acquire a significance beyond what they can actually deliver. This realization can be a source of great relief, since it also means that we cannot expect to devote more than a reasonable amount of time and effort to acquiring them.

We are thus freed to make space in our heads and hearts for the gifts that come from God, and for the freedom they bring: freedom from anxiety (less stress) and freedom from consuming desires (less time wasted in pursuing the things that damage our health and disrupt relationships, and which, in themselves, do not make for happiness).

This prayer or meditation has always suggested to me that trust is an activity that depends on having acquired (or at least wanting to acquire) this kind of freedom. It means being sufficiently free of physical, mental and emotional clutter to 'put down roots', and thus actively reach into God, who is the source of real wealth.

It can be helpful to reinforce this way of praying scripture with some kind of practical action. Why not plant a sturdy tree, bearing in mind how the young plant will flourish over the years, given the right conditions, and how its growth will not depend on its striving or being anxious about the next rainfall? It will simply get on with the business of growing, and so give glory to God.

Lorraine Cavanagh

I believe . . .

Lord, I believe, help thou mine unbelief.

Mark 9.24 (KJV)

Faith, we would all agree, is the greatest of gifts. It transforms our lives, giving them meaning and direction. Life will wound us, but it can never damage us; beneath all distress lies the reality of God.

It has always been a surprise to me that so many people regard this gift as offered only to the fortunate few. 'How I wish I had your faith,' they say wistfully. But faith is a gift offered to anyone. It is there for the taking. All we need to do is accept it.

What these hankerers after faith are seeking is not faith – freely given – but the feeling of faith, the conviction of faith, which is something quite other. An emotional experience is also a gift, but a passing one. It makes it easier to believe, but is otherwise wholly unimportant. Emotions pass: faith stays.

Nor can faith be proved. If we could prove our religion, then we would not need faith. It is not contrary to reason, but, as the Fathers of the Church have always said, faith comes first; understanding follows.

We believe by an act of the naked will. It is God who has drawn that will to himself, of course. Faith is given; it is grace. But giving is natural to our God; it is limited only by our unwillingness to receive. Tell him that you choose him, and all the implications of that choice as they will unfold for you, and you 'believe'. The immensity of that belief will take time to become clear to your mind, but the initial act accepts all that will flow from it. It is an act of supreme trust.

Here in the Gospels, we find the experience spelled out for us. Jesus has told the man that his child is healed. The father sees no proof. But he rallies his powers and chooses: 'Lord, I believe.' Then he faces, honestly, the differences between his words and his emotions. He does not feel belief. He feels unbelief. And, with the wisdom of the true child of God, he brings the problem to Jesus: 'Help thou mine unbelief.'

For most of us – there are exceptions – we must hold these two attitudes together in our hearts: a determination to believe and to act out that belief; and a sensation of non-belief.

For most people, there will be times when that sinking sense that it is all wishful thinking will be swept away by some blessed experience. Music, poetry, art, the silent beauty of an empty church, the rousing fervour of a full church, sermons preached from a heart that loves God . . . the list is endless. These graces are to be cherished, but never to be expected or needed. They are sweet extras. The basic act of faith is pure choice, pure reaction to God's gift.

It can be humbling to say this prayer. Unbelief is distasteful. But if we really believed, why are we not holy? We may think we have total faith (an emotional conviction, maybe), but if we were like St Paul, able to say genuinely, or better still to have said of us, that 'for me to live is Christ', then we, too, would be Pauline in spiritual stature.

There may be people who are indeed of that stature, and we thank God for their presence among us. But most of us will sadly confess that we do not love God as we desire; we do not love him enough. Why not?

Somewhere our faith is a non-faith. There are parts of us, subconscious perhaps, but inalienably ours, that do not accept Jesus fully. A holy priest I knew used to pray that God would heal that part of him that wanted no part of God. It distressed me to hear this said: I shudder to think there is that part of me. But surely it is there, or why no greater Jesus-fruit?

Sister Wendy Beckett

Thy will

Be it done to me according to thy will.

Luke 1.38

This always seems to me pure miracle: that a little Jewish nobody, barely into puberty (or she would have been married already), should be faced by God with such a question, and give such an answer.

In a small town, reputations matter. In agreeing to bear a child out of wedlock, Mary agreed to losing hers as a virginal young woman. She would have guessed that her husband-to-be, Joseph, would have to repudiate her. What future was there for an unmarried mother in those days, and a mother who knew, as nobody else would, that she was mother to the Holy One of God, his sole support?

In the event, it did not come to that. God sent Joseph a dream to reassure him, and Jesus was born to a married couple. But Mary did not have the gift of foreknowledge. Nevertheless, husband or not, the sheer weight of responsibility must have been terrifying. Yet she makes no plea for special help, supernatural guidance or miraculous vindication. She simply says: 'Fiat. I surrender to your will.'

In actuality, things will always be done to us 'according to his will'. We had no choice in where we were born or when; no choice in who our parents were, or what we inherited from them; no choice in the shaping of so much of our life. Even when things seemed up to us, and we did make radical choices, how often they were modified by accidental encounters – people, books, events.

Our vocation has always been to stand firm amid the unchosen, and direct our eyes to God. He is our choice. We often find, too, that things we have longed for, prayed for, perhaps schemed for, can disappoint, while the seeming disaster – whether a loss, or a failure, or an unhealed illness – can in the end turn out to be the greatest of blessings.

The difference between us and Mary is that we are dragged kicking and screaming into surrender, and then often half-heartedly, while she trusted her divine Father so absolutely that she gave herself at once, without fear or condition. She let him have his way, smilingly. But we, dour-faced 'trusters', still hold at base the conviction that our lives are safer if it is we who control them rather than God – even when all that happens proves it is not.

Mary could make this prayer of trust with such immediacy because she lived in trust. Prayer does not end when we rise from our knees or leave the church. Time has to be spent, serious time, alone with God, offering ourselves to him. But that intent time should lead us to the developing within us of an attitude. Saying that Yes 'that was always in Christ Jesus' (to quote St Paul) should be an instinct – just as a dancer, through long practice, will always move with elegance.

The Yes of Jesus was the instinctive response to the Father of a Son who loved him without reserve. We cannot even imagine Jesus deliberating, cost what it might; and the agony in the garden shows the extent of that cost. What was natural for Jesus is supernatural for Mary and for us, but it is a grace for the asking.

Fiat, fiat: we cannot pray this too often and too earnestly.

Sister Wendy Beckett

Worship

The Choristers' Prayer

Bless, O Lord, us thy servants
who minister in thy temple.
Grant that what we sing with our lips
we believe in our hearts,
And what we believe in our hearts
we may show forth in our lives;
through Jesus Christ our Lord.
Amen.

Anonymous, *Choristers' Pocket Book*

I am not the only ex-chorister who can remember the words of this prayer more easily than almost any other. From tiny chapels to great cathedrals, scores of singers use the Choristers' Prayer as both a final moment of reflection and as a liturgical full-stop, before they tear off their cassocks and lay aside the restraints of the worship in which they have just taken part.

My daughters were encouraged at school to collect in a notebook prayers that they found helpful. It is a good discipline. One of them chose this prayer, which appeared in the first edition of the *Choristers' Pocket Book*, published by the School of English Church Music in 1934. Despite being so well known, the prayer is not given an author. Some say it was written by the school's founder, Sir Sydney Nicholson, while others link it to Cosmo Gordon Lang, who became Archbishop of Canterbury in 1929.

The benefit of having an assortment of classic texts in our heads is obvious. Not only can we use them anywhere, but these prayers also help us to pray on days when our own words fail us and we need to lean on something familiar. Sometimes they are the only means by which the Spirit translates our incoherent groaning and gives it meaning.

I suspect the popularity of this prayer lies in its ability to reflect the question that is felt by all who regularly lead services: have I really entered into the spirit of worship, or have I just been doing what was written down for me as well as possible?

The use of set words and songs within the liturgy, the platform for the praise and intercession of Christians for 2000 years, always rides on the knife-edge between the dynamism of God's revelation on the one hand, and dull repetition and overfamiliarity on the other. So there is a healthy realism within the Choristers' Prayer. Most of us find it impossible to predict what will connect with us on any particular day, but we hope that, somewhere in the familiar, our attention will shift from our own concerns to an encounter with the living God.

Sometimes a prayer will work for us, while on another occasion it will leave us untouched. That, at least, is how we feel. And yet our outlook is fundamentally shaped by the prayers we use; they etch their way into our thinking. Just listen to the phrases used by those who are praying without a script: they are peppered with half-remembered lines from familiar prayers. And why not? Real prayers are not copyright.

Indeed, all set prayers are open to being adapted. Our church uses the Choristers' Prayer with the choir and the whole sanctuary party. So we pray together: 'Bless us, O Lord, and all who minister in your Holy Temple . . .'

It is a precious moment. Here, next to the faint sound of coffee cups being prepared, the music and the celebration are held for just 20 more seconds, before the candles are blown out and the liturgy of life takes over with a vengeance.

John Burniston

Such good things

Merciful God,
you have prepared for those who love you
such good things as pass our understanding:
pour into our hearts such love toward you
that we, loving you in all things and above all things,
may obtain your promises,
which exceed all that we can desire;
through Jesus Christ our Lord,
who is alive and reigns with you,
in the unity of the Holy Spirit,
one God, now and for ever.
Amen.

Collect for the 6th Sunday after Trinity, *Common Worship*

This is a prayer about the politics of love. We all know about the politics of fair distribution – the unseemly scrap over scarce resources, in which each of us fears we will be revealed as greedy, insecure, envious and deceitful. But this is a different kind of politics, the politics of things that really matter. Love, joy, peace . . . these things are not in short supply.

I can have large quantities of the world's limited resources, but, if I don't have kindness, goodness and gentleness, the other things are no good to me. Yet, if I have goodness, patience, self-control and the like, however much I have of the other things doesn't really matter. But this new world of love still involves politics – just politics of a different kind. Instead of carving up a limited cake, politics is now the shared discernment of the best use of the abundant gifts of God. But it is not the kind of game that only one team can win. My good no longer requires your loss. We have both learned to want the right things. And the right things, though their embodiment may be debated, don't have to be squabbled over: they are things that everyone can have.

There is a heresy that dominates our contemporary life. The heresy is that there is not enough. We live in the fourth richest country in the history of the world – and we still assume there is not enough. Not enough life, not enough food, not enough entertainment, not enough happiness. It's what keeps our economy going. We all assume we need more.

But the truth is the opposite. There is too much. We are overwhelmed, and our imaginations can't take it all in. There is limitless beauty for us to wonder at; there is so much truth to explore; there is so much goodness in the human spirit to admire. The archetypal heretic is the thief, since the temptation to steal is rooted in a perpetual fear that there will not be enough for oneself. When we trust that we will always have enough, we become generous. When we lose this trust, we become covetous and anxious.

The prayer begins and ends with an abundance of goodness. Yet, for a change, this is not the goodness of creation. It is the goodness of heaven, the goodness of restoration to the Father's presence, achieved through the ministry of the Son. When Jesus said: 'I am going to prepare a place for you' (John 14.2), this is what his promise meant.

But it is not just a theological statement. It is a prayer: it is worship. The key to the politics of love, the key to that limitless imagination that sees only abundance, that desires only the things that are not in short supply – that key lies in worship. For it is God who stretches and trains our imaginations; it is God's creation that trains us to look on the world with astonishment and wonder; and it is God's limitless love for us that inspires us to imagine that we and others could begin to love like that.

Sam Wells

The source of all holiness

Lord, you are holy indeed, the source of all holiness;
grant that by the power of your Holy Spirit,
and according to your holy will,
these gifts of bread and wine
may be to us the body and blood of our Lord Jesus Christ . . .

Holy Communion Order One:
Eucharistic Prayer B, *Common Worship*

Knowing a prayer really well and hearing it often is like driving a familiar route to and from work every day. You can do the whole thing on auto-pilot, without giving the matter in hand the attention it deserves – sometimes with damaging consequences.

Coasting through a liturgy isn't nearly such a risky business as driving without proper care; but it can leave us in danger of missing the force of what we are saying. In any case, these words are not so much a prayer as a little piece of one: an invocation of the Holy Spirit. It comes from Eucharistic Prayer B in *Common Worship*, a slightly revised form of the third eucharistic prayer in the *Alternative Service Book 1980*.

Though it is spoken by the priest alone, it can be used by individual worshippers as a prayer of preparation, an inspiring reminder of the wonder and power of the sacrament. Such a use can guard against the familiarity that breeds contempt, given that this prayer is prayed by priests, and given assent by congregations, week in, week out – be they high, low, or middle-of-the-road.

Like many prayers, it seems to be doing something odd: telling the Almighty who he is and what he is like. This is an aspect of prayer that puzzles non-Christians mightily. Why do we need to tell God that he is holy? In reality, we are doing something different in prayer: we are telling God that we recognize those qualities in him, that we acknowledge who and what he is.

So our prayer is not the futile ego-massage of a divine despot, but a complex interaction between members of a community and their leader. In prayers such as this, we reinforce our understanding of what binds us together; and, through the repetition of the words, we learn to recognize the qualities that mark God's presence and person.

There are many prayers that can do this. The reason these particular words are special is that they begin where we should always begin – with God's holiness. All things in our relationship with him depend on the recognition that God is holy.

Our first acceptance of that otherness of God may often come negatively, as a sense of falling short ('Just and holy is thy name; I am all unrighteousness; False and full of sin I am, Thou art full of truth and grace,' as Charles Wesley put it in 'Jesu, Lover of my soul'). But, to every mature Christian, there also comes a positive desire to become what God would have us be. In praying these words, we declare that the physical world is not mere matter, but that God is above all, and in all, and through all. We insist that wherever he is present, his presence makes ordinary things holy.

Four times in these few lines, the holiness of God is invoked; just before this, it has been given a threefold proclamation, 'Holy, holy, holy Lord'. Holiness is that which distinguishes the ordinary from the sacred, what has been charged with God's power and presence from what has not. When God is invoked in prayer, we need to remember that what we are doing is more than uttering a set phrase.

Here we ask for the Holy Spirit, working in accordance with God's holy will, to effect a change, making bread and wine something that previously they were not – the body and blood of our Lord. Dispute over the eucharistic species has gone on for centuries; it is ingrained in our identity as Christians of this Church or that. It is necessitated by our need to understand and classify what is happening before us on the altar, and to prescribe who may be entrusted with the privilege of acting as catalyst for the transformation.

Yet if we truly believe that God is holy indeed, and the source of all holiness, the transforming of the sacrament, and the real presence of Jesus in bread and wine are as easy to believe in as the rising of the sun on the morrow.

Cally Hammond

God's names

What can I say to you, my God?
Shall I collect together all the words that praise your holy name?
Shall I give you all the names of this world, you, the Unnameable?
Shall I call you 'God of my life, meaning of my existence,
hallowing of my acts, my journey's end, bitterness of my bitter hours,
home of my loneliness, you my most treasured happiness'?
Shall I say: Creator, Sustainer, Pardoner, Near One, Distant One,
Incomprehensible One, God both of flowers and stars,
God of the gentle wind and of terrible battles,
Wisdom, Power, Loyalty and Truthfulness, Eternity, and Infinity,
you the All-Merciful, you the Just One, you Love itself?

Karl Rahner (1904–84)

As may be expected from one of the twentieth century's greatest theologians, Karl Rahner's prayer is unlike most prayers, in that it never moves beyond the sheer immensity of God, and the near impossibility of getting beyond the necessary act of naming who it is who is being addressed.

Most prayers take it for granted that we know who God is. There is an assumption that the word 'God' is God's name, or that 'Lord' suffices. Rahner reminds us otherwise. He reminds us that we are engaged in the never-ending quest of identifying the Unnameable.

The prayer starts with an admission of surrender: 'What can I say to you, my God?' According to Rahner, we have only two alternatives: either to remain silent before God, aware of the inadequacy of our response to him, or to attempt to discover as much as we can of God by collecting 'together all the words that praise' his holy name as a way to come nearer to him.

Even then, Rahner recognizes the foolishness of the exercise, with the constant refrain of his question 'Shall I?' After all, they are merely all the words of this world. Who can possibly say how wonderful are the words with which the angels praise God?

What is so exciting about the prayer is the richness of the words that Rahner does use to praise God. Alongside, the 'meaning of [his] existence' and 'Eternal', 'Just' and 'Love itself', come 'the bitterness of [his] bitter hours', and the 'home of [his] loneliness'. For Rahner, not only do we owe our existence to God, but we are also maintained in existence by

God through God's continuing self-communication with us, whether or not we are conscious of him.

In that sense, everything we experience involves God. In our bitter hours and in our loneliness, God is not present as an impartial observer, but as part of their very texture. We are in a world in which God is an inescapable element: a God in whom 'we live and move and have our being' (Acts 17.28).

Such a God, though, is more mysterious than we might like. As Rahner's prayer acknowledges, such a God must be the God of 'flowers and stars', but also the God of 'terrible battles'. As a German Jesuit who lived through the Nazi era, Rahner's theology had to deal with the mystery of evil, a mystery that serves only to cast our God of Love into greater mystery. The prayer, however, doesn't evade it, although it cannot explain it. God is the 'Incomprehensible One', both the 'Near One' and the 'Distant One'.

It may seem odd that the name that is missing from the prayer is the Name 'that is above every name' (Philippians 2.9), Jesus. Rahner's personal devotion to Jesus was unquestionable. He understood Jesus, the Word, as God's definitive self-communication in human history, and the ultimate fullness of God's self-revelation. Yet he also argued that God's self-communication was implicit from the moment of creation through the Holy Spirit.

The prayer could be prayed by all humanity. It is a prayer that uses other words, such as 'Creator', 'Sustainer' and 'Pardoner', to convey the Trinity, and 'Near One' to reverence Christ. Yet it is a prayer founded in the mystery of loving God beyond our understanding.

Mark Speeks

Maintain the fabric

God of wholeness,
you have created us bodily,
that our work and faith may be one.
May we offer our worship
from lives of integrity;
and maintain the fabric of this world
with hearts that are set on you,
through Jesus Christ, Amen.

Janet Morley, collect for the 18th Sunday after
Pentecost, based on Ecclesiasticus 38.24–34,
from *All Desires Known*

In Guatemala, women traditionally wear a brightly coloured, square-cut blouse called a *huipil*. Made from woven cotton, it features birds, flowers and other local symbols. It takes a skilled worker about a week to weave, often on a very basic machine, made from something like an old bicycle wheel.

People say that you can tell where a woman is from because the complex series of pictures woven into the fabric forms a kind of pictogram address. If you know how to decipher it, the woven pictures can even tell you which house in a street in a given village she comes from.

Our English word 'text' comes from the Latin *texere*, which means to weave. When I read Janet Morley's collect for the 18th Sunday after Pentecost, and pray that our worship can help maintain the fabric of this world, I think of the texts of identity, belonging and meaning that those Guatemalan women weave into their clothing. I wonder what is woven into the text of my prayers and those of the congregation.

As happens in many other churches, our intercessions are a colourful hotchpotch of prayers for world events, for the peeling plaster on our walls, for the sick, for the Anglican Communion's deliberations about homosexuality, for the old people at the lunch club, for someone's granddaughter who has had a miscarriage, and for the ailing community transport minibus.

I would hate it if our prayers were so eloquently and loftily expressed that they could belong to any church community. I hope that, if visitors from the outside heard them, they would appreciate that they are a snap-shot of a real place and real people in their everyday concerns. These are people whose hearts are set on Jesus, and whose desire is to maintain the fabric of the world they know.

That fabric is woven together from the infinite number of encounters and relationships that make up our lives. Its text should be the address that locates us in God's world, as the Guatemalan women's *huipiles* locate them in theirs.

So this collect is a prayer that asks us to be honest and whole in our worship. It encourages us to bring our truest selves, complete though imperfect, and not to fragment ourselves, offering only the parts that we feel are acceptable. It steers us away from the veneers and generalizations that hide our real selves, and asks us simply to offer ourselves as we have been created.

By reminding us that our God is a God of wholeness, who has created us bodily, the collect pushes us collectively to allow each other the space to be real. It lets us name in worship those parts of our lives that we might find it hardest to love, or that the Church finds it hardest to let us talk about.

For me, this prayer is a good summary of what many of Janet Morley's prayers are about: engaging with the reality of our world, naming issues of gender and sexuality, and breathing new life into the stories of our faith. I want to belong to a Church that draws together the various strands of human experience, and weaves them into a fabric that glorifies God. This is a prayer that helps me to believe that that might be possible, and that shows me how to begin to do it.

Joanne Woolway Grenfell

Where angels sing

Lord, make my heart a place where angels sing!
For surely thoughts low-breathed by Thee
Are angels gliding near on noiseless wing;
And where a home they see
Swept clean, and garnish'd with adoring joy,
They enter in and dwell, and teach that heart to swell
With heavenly Melody, their own untried employ.

John Keble (1792–1866)

Having been born on the feast day of St Michael and all the Angels, I have always had a fascination with the angelic. The idea of angels existing just beyond our comprehension, bearing messages from God, and singing constant praises to God, is one of the delightful mysteries of our faith. This prayer, found for me by a friend, has captivated me with its imagery.

'Lord, make my heart a place where angels sing!' This wonderful opening line conjures up the possibility of heavenly music in the heart of our being. At times, our effort to rejoice in God, to offer praise and adoration, is clouded by all the weariness of our human life. Angels can offer unadulterated joyful worship, and this prayer seems to offer the possibility that they can sing that song in us and through us.

In Romans 8.26, Paul tells us that in response to suffering, our inarticulate groans are taken by the Spirit and expressed in prayer beyond words. Here we have the possibility that the delight and joy that we have no words for can be taken up in the singing of angels.

A member of my congregation in Sheffield, where I was the vicar, had advanced Parkinson's disease, and struggled to talk coherently. But he could still sing and play the piano. What he could not say in words he could sing in praise. Singing comes from a different part of the brain. This prayer encourages us to learn how to sing in our hearts, not ignoring the suffering and struggle of the world, but allowing ourselves to be lifted above it, delighting, for a moment, in the glory of God, caught up in the heavenly chorus.

Keble's angels are low-flying, gliding noiselessly, and ready to alight in the heart that is 'swept clean' and 'garnish'd with adoring joy'. This reminds us that we have a part to play. It is a call for us to keep our hearts clean and uncluttered. We need to sweep away the unkind and ungracious thoughts, and decorate our hearts with joy. It is to hearts open to the possibility of God's joyous love that angels will come to sing.

They will also do more than sing. They will teach us to sing and praise. Unless you are an accomplished and confident singer, it is easier to join in than to sing alone. It is also a wonderful experience to sing with those who can sing well. Angels singing within our heart can teach us to sing. Being open to the joyous praise of God can teach us to be joyful.

Angels are God's creatures whom we cannot compel, but we can ready our hearts, garnish them with joy, and pray that we may experience the delight of angels singing. In turn, our hearts may swell with heavenly melody.

Emma Percy

Calling

Thine

I am no longer my own, but thine.
Put me to what thou wilt,
rank me with whom thou wilt:
Put me to doing, put me to suffering:
Let me be employed for thee, or laid aside for thee:
Exalted for thee, or brought low for thee:
Let me be full, let me be empty:
Let me have all things, let me have nothing:
I freely and heartily yield all things
to thy pleasure and disposal.
And now, O glorious and blessed God,
Father, Son and Holy Spirit,
Thou art mine, and I am thine.
So be it.
And the covenant which I have made on earth,
let it be ratified in heaven.

John Wesley, The Methodist Covenant Prayer

This amazing prayer is a fitting reflection on John Wesley's conviction that Jesus offers to every person the chance of a living faith, and a personal relationship. His belief finds overwhelming expression here, in words that burn with the fire of love.

To pray this prayer is truly a form of self-abandonment to the divine providence. It stands in marked contrast to our wilful preference for keeping control over our lives: following that 'control freak' instinct; raging in anger whenever the world does not fit in with our plans and views, or value us as highly as we feel that we deserve.

The form of this prayer calls to mind a more familiar covenant, that of the marriage service. What else are wedding vows but a similar setting aside of the privacy of total individualism, committing oneself instead to fulfilment of the self through and with another? For better, for worse, for richer or poorer, in sickness or in health. The promise (if not always the reality) is one of committed, lasting, reliable love – the same love that is the basis of God's covenant with us.

This covenant prayer is often used at the beginning of a new year, a time of renewal, of new resolutions and new beginnings. But it speaks, each new year, of the oldest resolution of all – the agreement forged between God and his people. The rainbow was to be the eternal reminder of that bargain, and every time we see a rainbow, it reminds us of God's trustworthy, unbreakable covenant, his bond of everlasting love.

When I was a student, my parents made a covenant with me as a way of recovering the tax on the money they gave to support me. They expected nothing from me in return. They made the covenant because they loved me and wanted the best for me, but they did not demand reciprocity. They simply hoped for it. What's more, it had to be renewed regularly, or it became void.

The same is true of our covenant with God – we need to commit ourselves to his service, and pledge our trust in his love, regularly. Otherwise, the covenant becomes void. This prayer is designed for that purpose. And God makes his side of the bargain in the hope, not the demand, that we will respond.

Two points in the prayer stand out. First, the intention that we yield our lives freely and heartily. St Paul wrote that God loves a cheerful giver, not a grudging one. He wants us to act as we are disposed in our heart, not from necessity. To pray these words is to make an old-fashioned act of will, that by the grace of God we shall be freed from the cold, corrosive chains of ambition, anxiety and acclaim, which we can never escape by our own efforts.

Second, the last words show that this prayer is only one half of a dialogue. As we pray it, we end by expressing trust in the answering pledge that makes the covenant binding. Exactly how that answering pledge will come, we must each discover for ourselves, but that it will come to each of us, we no more need doubt than did John Wesley.

Cally Hammond

The Angelus

The angel of the Lord brought tidings unto Mary:
and she conceived by the Holy Ghost.

Hail Mary, full of grace, the Lord is with thee;
blessed art thou among women and blessed is the fruit of
thy womb, Jesus;
holy Mary, Mother of God, pray for us sinners
now and at the hour of our death.

Behold the handmaid of the Lord:
be it unto me according to thy word.

Hail Mary . . .

And the Word was made flesh: and dwelt among us.

Hail Mary . . .

Pray for us, O holy Mother of God:
that we may be made worthy of the promises of Christ.

We beseech thee, O Lord, pour thy grace into our hearts:
that, as we have known the incarnation of thy Son Jesus Christ
by the message of an angel, so by his cross and Passion we may
be brought unto the glory of his resurrection; through the same
Jesus Christ our Lord. Amen.

You might think this prayer is for Roman Catholics. At first, it seems
a straightforward devotion to Mary. And, to paraphrase Alan Bennett:
'We're Church of England; we don't do that kind of thing.' Yet, apart
from the Lord's Prayer, the Angelus is the most scriptural and affirming
prayer that I know.

As a celebration of the incarnation, it can be used at any time. Those
words 'Hail Mary, full of grace, the Lord is with thee' are spoken by the
angel Gabriel (hence Angelus) at Luke 1.28, and they mark the moment
in human history when the miracle of the good news – God's becoming
like us to make us like him – was first declared.

The scripture we think of first in connection with the incarnation is
from St John: 'The Word was made flesh: and dwelt among us' (John
1.14) – and it has a place within this prayer. But the focus is on Gabriel's

words to Mary, who stands for the whole human race, among whom the Lord chooses to make his home.

The Hail Mary forms part of other devotions – it is a prayer in its own right. Its modern form has three parts, the first two being the words of Gabriel and Elizabeth respectively (from Luke 1.26, 28, 42, with the addition of the names of Mary and Jesus). The third part ('Holy Mary . . .') is potentially more problematic, being non-scriptural. It came later, and was probably adapted from a litany of the saints ('Holy N, pray for us') or the Office of Mary. Anglicans uncomfortable with this part of the prayer could substitute, 'Mother of Christ'.

The origins of the Angelus go back at least 800 years, to the custom of praying the Hail Mary three times on hearing the evening (compline) bell; evening was the time when the annunciation was thought to have taken place. Later, the prayer was linked with the morning bell at the time when the resurrection took place. The noonday Angelus came later, and is associated with the Passion, as well as with prayer for peace.

By the 1500s, the Angelus was appearing in various prayer books in its present form. The nascent Church of England gave up ringing the aves ('hails') on Cranmer's instructions. On the other hand, it was Cranmer who rescued the closing prayer of the Angelus, and included it in the Book of Common Prayer of 1549, as the collect for the feast of the Annunciation.

This collect still has an official place in Anglican worship today. It links the three themes of incarnation, Passion and resurrection, to which the whole prayer bears witness (three aves prayed three times daily).

Part of the power of the Angelus lies in its perfect theological proportions – in the Hail Marys, two parts acclamation to one part intercession ('pray for us'). Part lies in the clarity of focus, reinforced by the versicles and responses, on the moment of incarnation when God became Emmanuel: God-with-us.

Part lies, too, in its flexibility. I have been praying the Angelus for nearly 20 years, since I went as a student to a church where it was customary to end the Sunday service by singing it. I find it often the first prayer to rise to my lips in the morning, or late at night, or when I am too tired or low to pray anything else, or simply cannot find words of my own. Perhaps this is because it is so hopeful, without stating specific objects.

Some churches ring an Angelus bell – morning, noon and evening – to mark the times of the resurrection, Passion and annunciation. The bell's significance goes often unnoticed – rather like the incarnation itself. Yet the reality of the Angelus, and of the incarnation to which it testifies, is all around us, for those blessed with eyes to see how God has written himself into the fabric of his world, and on our hearts and minds.

Cally Hammond

Give us priests

Almighty God, give us priests:
to establish the honour of your holy name;
to offer the holy sacrifice of the altar;
to give us Jesus in the holy sacrament;
to proclaim the faith of Jesus;
to tend your sheep;
to seek the lost;
to give pardon to the penitent sinner;
to bless our homes;
to pray for the afflicted;
to comfort mourners;
to strengthen us in our last hour;
to commend our souls;
Almighty God, give us priests!

The Additional Curates Society Prayer

Writing about the abolition of the post of Lord Chancellor, a journalist in the *Guardian* made the observation that 'heavy, silly or restrictive costumes are important, because they give the wearer a sense of the weight of responsibility of their position'. Newly ordained priests might also come to terms with that perception.

This prayer brilliantly captures the multifaceted nature of priestly ministry. It also necessarily and inevitably illuminates the experience, needs and mission of lay people, and in that sense is their prayer.

During the past decade, division over the ordained ministry seems to have sapped our confidence and enthusiasm for praying for and fostering priestly vocations. This must be to the detriment of the life of the people of God. The Church needs priests, not to sustain its structures, but to dispense wisely and sensitively the refreshing channels of grace for an age that thirsts for authenticity more acutely than it cares about authority.

In this prayer, the ministry that is described clearly points to the High Priest, Jesus Christ. Those who are asked to bear for him the task of exercising what is only and ever his, do so not in their own strength, but by his grace alone.

When a priest puts on the vestments for the celebration of the eucharist, there are prayers to be said for each one as a reminder of the weight of responsibility to which they point.

The concept of putting on sacred vestments is essential to the scriptural understanding of priesthood. Just as the High Priest of the Old Covenant put on vestments representing the material creation in order to minister in the Temple, so the High Priest of the New Covenant, Jesus, assumes our earthly nature in order to enter heaven redemptively on our behalf.

But the Gospel accounts of the redemptive, healing ministry of Jesus do not result in dependency, but in discipleship. After meeting Jesus, the woman at the well 'hurried back to tell the people, "Come and see . . ."' In response to a request to stay with Jesus, the man called Legion was gently told: 'Go home to your people and tell them all that the Lord in his mercy has done for you.'

The confidence with which we pray for an increase of vocations to the priesthood should reflect this perception. Exercise of the ministry of Jesus Christ, the High Priest, is more than external vesture. The authenticity with which they are worn is evident not in the promotion of self-serving authority and dependency, but in the joyful growth of the flock in dignity and holiness, and freedom for mission.

You could pray this prayer, first in thanksgiving for your parish priest, and second in renewal of your discipleship and witness.

Martin Warner

Constituted by prayer

Dear Jesus, send your Spirit on us so that we will be taught to pray.
Prayer is hard, requiring great effort, but when done, effortless.
I confess I have never liked to pray.
Prayer is too much like begging.
So I have to pray that your generous Spirit will teach me to beg.
I beg you to help all of us discover that our lives are constituted by
  prayer,
so that we may be in your world one mighty, joyous prayer.
Make us so rested by such prayer, so content to be your people, that we
  kill no more. Amen.

Stanley Hauerwas, from Prayers Plainly Spoken

Growing up as a Methodist in Texas, Stanley Hauerwas took it for granted that someone in his family would naturally have the gift of prayer. His father assumed the mantle for many years. The gift of prayer was taken to be genetic, and Stanley was supposed to inherit the gift. His problems began when he discovered that he hadn't.

The prayers of the Church were one thing. Their rhythm shaped his life. But his own prayers were quite another. He was a world-famous theologian by the time that, aged 50 and newly married, he was asked by his wife if he prayed before his lectures. For sure, he had a host of reflex reasons why he didn't. But none of them matched up. So now he does.

His prayers are not 'holy'. He loathes what he calls 'piety', which he associates with a fanciful sentimentality. Like the psalmist, he speaks plainly: God does not need protection from the truth. He does not concentrate on correct forms of speech: there is no striving after the cadences of praise and petition to be found in a prayer book collect. Instead, he shares his thoughts with God, with a jarring ingenuousness that precludes complacency.

This prayer, 'Teach me to beg', expresses these convictions. Like many, perhaps most, Christians, Stanley knows that prayer doesn't come naturally. But he seeks the ministry of the Spirit, that what is not nature may be seared into the soul through habit, and thus become second nature. It will always be work, but, in time, it will become effortless work.

The heart of prayer is recognizing, embodying, practising dependence on God – and finding that this service expresses and empowers perfect freedom. But, to discover this, one has to learn how to beg. The biggest obstacle to prayer is not philosophical misgivings nor lack of time nor a buzzing mind; it is simply pride, the reluctance to beg. So, a second time, the ministry of the Spirit is invoked to subvert such pride.

The prayer is that life becomes a prayer. I know a person who learned to read, in her fifties, by reading the Bible to those who met on a Sunday to share evening prayer. After a year or so, she started to lead prayers on odd Sundays, in the same way, out of the prayer book. One day, a year or so later, the person due to read prayers was not there. There was no prayer book to hand. There was a pause. 'I'll do it,' she said, and began to put together sentences, half-remembered liturgical phrases blending with the language of the heart. Habit nurtured had become second nature.

Do the last three words of this prayer shock? They remind us that non-violence is not just an option paraded by the plaintive on the eve of war. It is at the heart of faith and discipleship or it is nowhere. Stanley is a violent man made peaceable by the rugged disciplines of sacrament and service. Peace comes only through the cross and resurrection of Christ; and the way to shape our lives around the cross is through prayer.

Sam Wells

Live in thy servants

O Jesus, living in Mary,
Come and live in thy servants,
In the spirit of thy sanctity,
In the fullness of thy strength,
In the reality of thy virtues,
In the perfection of thy ways,
In the communion of thy mysteries.
Be Lord over every opposing power,
In thine own Spirit,
To the glory of the Father. Amen.

Jean-Jacques Olier (1608–57),
founder of the seminary of Saint-Sulpice

Jean-Jacques Olier was one of a remarkable group of priests who dedicated themselves to the revival of priestly formation in seventeenth-century France. When he began his work, it was unusual for even the most serious of candidates to have anything more than a few weeks' retreat to prepare themselves for ordination. By the time of his death, he had established the sort of seminary training familiar in our own times. His methods were the inspiration for many of the Tractarians, and the influence of Saint-Sulpice was especially strong among those trained at Cuddesdon: this prayer has found its way into Anglican spirituality through its inclusion in *The Cuddesdon Office Book*.

Olier inherited from the founder of the French school of spirituality, Cardinal Pierre de Bérulle, a great devotion to the interior life of Christ: their inspiration was the teaching of St Paul in Galatians 2.20: 'It is no longer I who live, but Christ who lives in me.' Indeed, he placed so much emphasis when preaching on 'putting to death the old man' that the elderly gardener of the seminary became convinced he was about to be murdered. At the heart of Olier's teaching was the need for the Christian to imitate Christ not simply in word and in deed, but by a real participation in the continuous self-offering of the incarnation.

The prayer begins strikingly: 'O Jesus, living in Mary'. Olier was devoted to the mother of Jesus, and in the country retreat of Saint-Sulpice at Issy there was a chapel built to resemble the Holy House at Nazareth, similar to the one at Walsingham. But he knew that true devotion to the saints is really devotion to the life of Christ lived in them, which is why he prays that what Mary has, as the one who most perfectly does the will of God, might be given to every Christian.

The main part of the prayer is a meditation on what the life of Christ within the Christian might be. At Saint-Sulpice, one of the high points of the liturgical year was the feast day set aside to honour the interior life of Jesus. The prayer takes up this theme, and makes of it a petition: the Christian is called not simply to know Christ as he spoke and acted in the Gospels, but to share in what the leaders of the French school loved to call his states, the moral and spiritual perfections of his human life, which continue in the glory of the resurrection.

Olier concludes by relating the life of Christ in the Christian to 'the glory of the Father'. His mentor Bérulle taught that the whole incarnate life of Jesus was an offering of perfect worship to the Father, culminating in the cross and continued in the eucharist. Our worship of the Father is only acceptable, only able to give glory, in so far as it is the work of Christ offering himself within us.

Robin Ward

The Master Carpenter's Prayer

O Christ, the Master Carpenter,
who at the last, through wood and nails,
purchased our whole salvation:
wield well your tools in the workshop of your world,
so that we who come rough-hewn to your bench may here
    be fashioned to a truer beauty of your hand.
We ask it for your own name's sake. Amen.

Arthur Gray, used in *The Iona Community Worship Book*

As associate members of the Iona Community, my wife and I make this prayer daily, as part of the Community's Office. We have known and valued it for more than 50 years. It was used in our parish church in Leeds in the 1950s as a congregational prayer at the end of the parish communion.

In the prayer, we speak to Christ as a carpenter, a special kind of artist. Eric Gill (1882–1940) was one of the most versatile artists of the twentieth century: typographer, graphic artist, letter-carver, sculptor and engraver. He used to insist: 'An artist is not a special kind of person, but every person is a special kind of artist.'

I have no skills with the tools of carpentry, but I have been trained as a mechanic and fitter. I was taught to use drills, micrometers, files, hacksaws and pressure gauges. In a small way, I can make things, adapt and repair things. So can cooks, knitters, accountants and gardeners.

In our prayer, we ask Christ to make us, modify and repair us, using the tools by which the Creator works the creation. What tools? We are made by genetics, environment, schooling, economic forces. We offer ourselves to be shaped by the Creator, using the tools of creation. We ask that these tools be good and true, according to their design. We ask this for our children, our neighbours and our enemies.

We ourselves are also tools, for the shaping and reshaping of each other. We offer ourselves to be used by Christ the artist. The artist can look at us and see potential. The artist can improvise; can see what might be done with this piece of seven-ply, this fleece, this area of ground, this reserve of funds (Jesus may have been a carpenter, but, judging from his parables, the subjects that really switched him on at school were botany and economics).

Seeing potential is creativity. Hydrogen is a light, colourless gas, which given sufficient time (say, 15 billion years) can become the Archbishop of Canterbury. This is potential. We share in the process of enabling each other to become what we are intended to be.

There was a condition attached to Eric Gill's remark about artists. His precise words were: 'In a normal society, one, that is to say, composed of persons who are responsible for what they do and for what they make, the artist is not a special kind of man, but every man is a special kind of artist.'

For the most part, we are not in a normal society in this world. Many are excluded, disallowed from personal responsibility. But this was the world that Jesus took as his workshop, in a voteless community of non-citizens.

He used wood and nails not just to make an elegant table, but in the process of our salvation. The instrument constructed of wood and nails was designed to state that he was a convicted terrorist – expendable, rubbish, superfluous to the world's requirements. It put him alongside everyone who is treated as dis-abled, excluded, problematic. He took a process that was supremely untrue, and turned it to truth.

Truth, at this point, is not a matter of getting the words right, but truth in a mechanic's or an architect's sense: the truth of a surface that is not distorted, or of a bridge that is up to its job. Christ used wood and nails, not to construct something outside himself, but to enable himself to be used for our repairing.

In this prayer we offer ourselves, day by day, to be artists with Christ, sharers in this process of making and repairing, of recreating a 'normal' world.

John D. Davies

Called by name

God of life and love,
whose risen Son called Mary Magdalene by name
and sent her to tell of his resurrection to his apostles:
in your mercy, help us,
who have been united with him in this eucharist,
to proclaim the good news
   that he is alive and reigns, now and for ever.

Post-communion for Mary Magdalene (22 July),
Common Worship

Mary Magdalene could be thought of as the patron saint of the Much Maligned. For centuries, she has been depicted as the scarlet woman, the 'tart with a heart' who abandoned a life of prostitution to follow Jesus.

In the musical *Jesus Christ Superstar* she sings of Jesus: 'I've had so many men before in very many ways: he's just one more.' In the film *The Last Temptation of Christ* she is introduced to us in her bed, and it is to her that Jesus' mind wanders during the crucifixion. Such imagery has proved undeniably powerful, but has no scriptural basis.

St Luke mentions 'some women who had been healed of evil spirits and infirmities', among them, 'Mary, called Magdalene, from whom seven demons had gone out' (Luke 8.2). Elsewhere in the Gospels, an un-named woman washes Jesus' feet with her tears and wipes them with her hair – a scandalous but loving and generous act. It has traditionally been assumed that she is Mary Magdalene. She is thus confirmed as a woman who loved Jesus dearly and as someone who knew the power of sensual-ity and her own sexuality.

Thankfully, this prayer ignores the unfounded tradition. Instead, it recognizes that even if we know nothing else about Mary, we know this: it was she who first saw the risen Lord, and it was to Mary that Jesus gave the apostolic commission: 'Go to my disciples . . . and tell them' (John 20.17).

The prayer reminds us that she was called by name. In John's account of the resurrection, Jesus does indeed call her by her name. When she mistakes him for the gardener, he turns to her and says, 'Mary'. It is one of those moments that never fails to make the hairs on my neck stand up, because it is the saying of her name that causes her to see who he really is. The scales of grief fall from her eyes. It is Jesus, her Lord, alive before her when she expected to find him dead.

More importantly, it is the saying of her name that opens her eyes to the resurrection and its meaning. It takes us back right to the creation in Genesis where, in order to bring something into life, God names it. And it takes us on to the baptism service, in which the candidate is brought into the resurrection life by being named. Jesus said, 'Mary', and she became alive.

More than this, the word 'called' in this prayer reminds us that Jesus not only said her name aloud, but he also called her to a task, a vocation – to go and tell his disciples about the resurrection. Being part of the resurrection meant sharing the good news, telling others that Jesus was risen from the dead.

The prayer ends by weaving her calling into our own calling. It is a post-communion prayer, and as such sends us out from the church and back to the world. We who have been brought near to Jesus Christ in the eucharist are called into the new life of the resurrection.

We who have been united with his body and blood are called to open our eyes to who he is – even when we encounter him in unexpected places. And we, who like Mary have reached out and touched him, are called with her to depart and proclaim the good news.

Georgina Byrne

Work silently within my heart

Holy Spirit, giver of life,
who didst overshadow Mary that she might become
   the mother of Jesus Christ our Saviour,
do thou likewise work silently within my heart
to form within me the fullness of his redeemed
and redeeming humanity.
Give me a share in his loving heart to burn with love for
   God and love for people.
Give me a share in his joy and his sorrow,
his weakness and his strength,
his labour for the world's salvation.
May Mary, blessed among women, mother of our Saviour,
pray for me that Christ may be formed in me,
that I may live in union of heart and will
   with Jesus Christ her Son, our Lord and Saviour. Amen.

Cheslyn Jones (1918–87)

Here is a prayer to the Holy Spirit, 'the Lord, the giver of life', that we may grow more Christ-like. The prayer's basic conviction is that the life of our Lord and Saviour is lived in the lives of Christians. St Paul tells us that 'you have died and now the life you have is hidden with Christ in God' (Colossians 3.3); he reminds us of 'Christ among you, your hope of glory' (Colossians 1.27). There are commandments, precepts and spiritual duties, but essentially our faith is a life lived.

This prayer originated as a petition offered by a priest for himself, and also intended for use by ordinands in training. It can, of course, be appropriately uttered by anyone. Phrase after phrase can be used as starting points for reflection or further prayer.

Canon Cheslyn Jones composed this prayer at the now defunct Chichester Theological College, of which he was the Principal from 1956 to 1970. As a former student there, I remember him with affectionate thanksgiving. A man of learning, with something of the monk about him, Cheslyn also came across as an unfulfilled cabaret artist at the piano. He had a ready sense of humour, and a perception of the burdens of life, but one learned most from hearing him talk about St John's Gospel or observing his recollection in celebrating mass. In later life he had a bad press as Principal of Pusey House, Oxford, but I am grateful for his memory, and greatly appreciate his prayer.

Its quiet reference to our Lady reflects Cheslyn's complaint on one occasion that some of the students believed a great deal too much about her, but others not nearly enough. We were a very mixed bunch.

In ordinary weeks and ways, Christ's life is to be lived out by the faithful: so we pray for growth in Christ-like character. He makes our joys and sorrows his, and we, in some measure, share his in our own. This reciprocation leads the one who prays into exploration of what gives the resurrected Jesus joy or sorrow now. It makes sensitive our concern for God's world and Christ's Church. The Christ life is a call to new concerns and unexpected cares. Thus to let the Holy Spirit 'work silently within my heart' is not just gratifying self-culture, but the receiving of the dangerous gift of 'a share in [Jesus'] loving heart'.

The Holy Spirit brought about the incarnation of our Lord: now we pray that the Holy Spirit, whose life we share in the Holy Church through baptism and the laying-on of hands, may work in us to make us Christ-like; his life developing in us. We ask Mary's prayers in the communion of saints that that work may be forwarded. To that end, the Christian offers 'heart and will'.

John Gaskell

The fruit of silence

The fruit of silence is PRAYER.
The fruit of prayer is FAITH.
The fruit of faith is LOVE.
The fruit of love is SERVICE.
The fruit of service is PEACE.

The Blessed Teresa of Calcutta
(Mother Teresa) (1910–97)

On 10 September 1946, during a train journey from Calcutta to Darjeeling, Mother Teresa received what she later described as 'a call within a call' to find and serve Jesus in those she referred to as 'the unwanted, the unloved, and the uncared-for'.

Over the next 50 years, this vocation bore fruit in the work of the Missionaries of Charity. By 1997, the Sisters of Charity alone numbered nearly 4,000 members, and the order had houses in 123 countries from Cuba to Tanzania. Teresa had borne lasting fruit.

Teresa believed that she had received a commission to be the light of Christ to the poor. In 1995, a compendium of interviews and writings was published entitled *A Simple Path* (Rider & Co.). This prayer is the outline of her simple path. The closer Teresa became to Jesus through prayer, the more she found that she had to respond to the love of Jesus in action for the poorest of the poor.

This prayer, moving from silence to service, is a summary of the Christian life. Silence and service both played a part in Mother Teresa's life: silence, as a religious who waited on God; and service, as she waited on other people. Here, Teresa highlights an essential truth – that prayer and the practical outworking of the Christian faith are intimately linked.

Christian action can only ever spring from the love and faith that are rooted in prayer. The conscious relationship with God that we nurture through prayer spills over into how we deal with other people. So we can have more confidence in what we do if our actions are characterized by the wisdom that springs from prayer, faith and love.

These qualities of the Christian life do not exist in a hermetically sealed vacuum, and should not be seen as ends in themselves – rather, they inform each other, and ultimately lead to the peace that is found in doing

God's will and in sharing his life. Service, then, finds its own fruit in God's peace.

Why is this? In Matthew's Gospel, Jesus tells his hearers that whenever they fed, welcomed, clothed, or cared for one of the least of his brothers and sisters, it was as if they did it to him (Matthew 25.31–46). In serving others, especially those who are 'the poorest of the poor', we bear fruit, and thus find our true peace with the one who came not to be served but to serve.

When the leaders of the G8 group of countries met in July 2005, parts of the press derided the Make Poverty History campaign as 'tokenistic' or 'too idealistic'. But this was to miss the point. Social action is not an optional extra for the Christian – whether it be in supporting the work of Amnesty or Christian Aid, or consecrating one's life to the poor on the streets of Calcutta. Such action is the fruit of loving, prayerful living, which has its roots in the endlessly creative silence of God's heart.

Those of us who are fortunate enough to enjoy clean water, health care and the protection of our civil rights enshrined in law have much to be thankful for. But the Swiss theologian Hans Urs von Balthasar wrote that it is not thankfulness that God wants, but fruitfulness.

Thankfulness can prove that it is truly Christian only by bringing fruit. The pilgrimage of the Christian faith is a journey of fruition – but, to bring forth good fruit, we need to tend and prune our praying, loving and believing, so that we can serve God in our impoverished brothers and sisters, and in our impoverished communities.

This hopeful prayer shows us the qualities we will need to live the Christian life fruitfully. As Christ told us, we are commissioned to bear fruit that will last.

Jamie Hawkey

Saviour

Jesus, Jesus, be to me a Jesus.

Anonymous

The point of this prayer, as we know from the Catechism, is that the holy name 'Jesus' means 'saviour'. The words are simple, and so is the concept, but it is a profound simplicity, the dimensions of which are beyond our full comprehension. There are no words that define God. He eludes all comprehension. What we comprehend, enclose in our minds, come to intellectual terms with, by definition cannot be God.

Jesus is Saviour: from what? Every human creature knows neediness. None of us is sufficient to ourselves. We always reach out for that fullness of life, that integrity of personality, that inner rightness for which we know we are made.

We long to be saved from inadequacy. Life is short enough without moving through it wastefully: at best impervious to imperfection or disaster, at worst damaged by them. Never to enter totally into happiness, only fleetingly, if at all, to respond to the wonder of the world; from these incompletions and failures, we pray to be saved.

In many cultures, that of the Old Testament among them, naming confers power. If we know another's name, we have a hand on his essence. Sometimes this power was feared; within the family, there was for each child a secret name, with another for the outer world.

The implication is a sad one: one is safe only with one's own. So there can seem a sort of lavish trustfulness in the openness with which we are made free of the name of God's Son. 'His name shall be called Jesus.'

Knowing a name does indeed confer power. We can call him and be certain that he will answer, though that answer is a silent one. Only God, only Jesus, really knows our own name, that defining name that expresses completely what we are. We are promised that in heaven God will greet us with that name, revealing to us what he has always known, the mystery of our uniqueness.

The prayer I have chosen, short though it is, could be even shorter: its only essential element is the holy name. Even to say that name is a profound act, taking us out of the everyday, where we cope well or as best we can, and into the eternal, where all is mystery and we have only to let ourselves be loved. There is a sacredness about the personal element here, actually calling to our Saviour by his name, a mark of intimacy that he gladly offers, but of which we feel unworthy.

He is Jesus. You are . . . whoever you are: John, Alice, David . . . You call; he turns to you. Who can understand that wonder?

Sister Wendy Beckett

Speak, Lord

Speak, Lord, for your servant is listening.

1 Samuel 3.9

The Old Testament has numerous comic moments. One of my favourites is the passage from which this quotation is taken. In the well-known story, the infant Samuel, who is sleeping in the temple, hears a voice calling. Samuel, with childlike innocence, jumps up three times, but, as children do, remains unperturbed when each time Eli declares that he hasn't spoken.

The repetition almost turns it into a game; perhaps Samuel believes that if he keeps going, Eli will admit that he has been teasing him all along. Samuel takes the voice at face value, but lacks the ability to interpret what it might mean.

Eli, on the other hand, is depicted as a bewildered elderly man with failing eyesight, who is woken twice before he works out what is going on. Anyone who is woken three or so times in a single night might have sympathy for him – it is remarkable that, on the third waking, he works out what is happening, and gives Samuel the words with which he can respond.

Samuel is fortunate to have on hand a guide such as Eli. Although there are problems with Eli (as becomes clear from what God says to Samuel in 1 Samuel 3.12–14), even in a sleepy befuddled state, Eli was able to give Samuel words that allowed him to hear and respond to God's call. Although Eli's physical eyesight was failing, his spiritual eyesight was not, leading him unerringly to these words that, though simple, contain a world of meaning.

Many people have favourite words that help them to enter into prayer; these are mine. They provide an ideal introduction to prayer: they invite God to communicate with us ('Speak, Lord'); they establish a relationship ('your servant' – though, in the light of the New Testament, we might change this to 'child' or 'friend'); and undertake to respond ('is listening' – the Hebrew can have the emphasis of understanding or of listening with interest). These three – invitation, relationship and response – lie at the heart of prayer.

Of course, saying them and meaning them are two different things.

I cannot help wondering whether Samuel regretted uttering these words. Poor Samuel was faced with telling Eli that his family was corrupt and about to be destroyed by God. If we utter these words and mean them, there is a high likelihood that, at some point, God will give us a task as difficult as Samuel's was. At the same time, however, the message to Samuel promised such divine action in the world that it would make 'make both ears of anyone who hears of it tingle' (1 Samuel 3.11).

If we utter Samuel's simple prayer, we risk hearing what God really wants to say to us, our world and our churches. While this might well be a difficult message, it can communicate the ear-tingling action of God to the world. The story of Samuel and Eli attaches a powerful warning to these words. Pray them if you dare.

Paula Gooder

Wisdom and justice

Know the difference

God, grant us grace to accept
the things we cannot change,
Courage to change the things
we can change,
And wisdom to know the difference.

Reinhold Niebuhr (1892–1971)

Reinhold Niebuhr is unusual among academic theologians for having served a substantial pastorate, at Bethel Evangelical Church in Detroit from 1915 to 1928. This experience was formative of a great deal that followed when teaching at the Union Theological Seminary in New York.

In his *Leaves from the Note-book of a Tamed Cynic* (forgive the language, it was published in 1929), he wrote:

> If a minister wants to be a man among men he need only stop creating devotion to abstract ideals which everyone accepts in theory and denies in practice, and to agonize about their validity and practicability in the social issues which he and others face in our present civilization. That immediately gives his ministry a touch of reality and potency.

Against the prevailing liberal theology of his day, Niebuhr emphasized human sinfulness and our capacity for self-deception. In his view, contemporary culture under-emphasized the demonic force of human life. According to Niebuhr, the crucifixion demonstrated that 'sin is so much a part of existence that sinlessness cannot maintain itself within it'.

Yet Niebuhr was no pessimist. He believed that people could deal constructively with their problems if they relied on grace and forsook illusions. This prayer exemplifies both Niebuhr's realism and his hope.

As a pastor, Niebuhr was in the habit of praying extempore during services. One Sunday in 1932, he was asked for a copy of one of his prayers, but as it wasn't written down he struggled to reconstruct it. Sometimes other people spot the significance and worth of things we say better than we do ourselves.

The prayer was first published in 1934, and in its short version is now much loved and well used. The full version is less well known. It continues:

> Living one day at a time,
> enjoying one moment at a time,
> accepting hardship as the pathway to peace;
> taking, as He did, this sinful world as it is,
> not as I would have it;
> trusting that He will make all things right if I surrender to His will;
> that I may be reasonably happy in this life,
> and supremely happy with Him for ever in the next. Amen.

A friend who has been struggling with the consequences of addiction in his family recently was struck by a sentence in Evelyn Anthony's novel *The Legacy*: 'Show me an addict and you will show me a manipulator and a liar.' If that statement is true, it is easy to see why the short version of this prayer was given to Alcoholics Anonymous (AA) in 1939, and was so readily accepted by Bill Wilson, one of their co-founders.

Here is a prayer longing for reality, acceptance, courage and wisdom. It knows our need to change, and that some change is beyond us. The success of the AA programme is, in part, in its recognition that everyone needs faith in God, however God is conceived.

Niebuhr's prayer reminds us of our condition, suspended as we are between the poles of wretchedness and glory. He recognizes that salvation is not in our own hands, but that we are called to live in response to the fact of our salvation, and not in our strength alone.

Nicholas Holtam

Open my eyes

O Lord, open my eyes
that I may see the need of others,
open my ears
that I may hear their cries,
open my heart
so that they need not be without succour.
Let me not be afraid to defend the weak
because of the anger of the strong,
nor afraid to defend the poor
because of the anger of the rich.
Show me where love and hope and faith are needed,
and use me to bring them to these places.
Open my eyes and ears
that I may, this coming day,
be able to do some work of peace for thee.

Alan Paton (1903–88)

Born out of the misery of apartheid South Africa, this prayer has a time-less quality. It speaks to the heart of our humanity, recognizing the tension within us between desiring safety and risk, between looking after ourselves and reaching out to others. And it gently challenges us to acknowledge the help we need.

Underlying its words is the belief that, without God, we remain closed to the world, and that such self-sufficiency not only impoverishes those we neglect, but diminishes us also. Being open to God and being open to others go hand in hand.

I first learned this from my father, which perhaps is why this prayer resonates with me. For him, prayer was about relationship – his relationship with God, and his relationship with the world. Every night, he knelt by his bed to pray, but his words didn't end there. They informed his encounters with the people he met: the tramp who went away wearing my father's suit; institutionalized Doris, who learned to read and write at our kitchen table; tall, lonely Eric, a convicted paedophile. My father's eyes were open to each of them, precisely because he recognized his own need of his maker.

Alan Paton's expression of this triangular relationship between God, us, and our neighbour echoes the passage from Isaiah read by Jesus at the outset of his ministry: 'The Spirit of the Lord is upon me, because he has anointed me to bring good news to the poor. He has sent me to proclaim release to the captives and recovery of sight to the blind' (Isaiah 61.1; Luke 4.18). Conversely, however, it is our own blindness to which his prayer alludes. But, with renewed vision, comes a defining moment. Do we retreat, or do we seek courage and enter a world of conflict, where the struggles of the poor become our own?

The fear that this prayer articulates is tangible and compelling. Having its roots in one man's struggle to speak out against a regime that systematically oppressed the poor black majority and elevated the interests of a rich and powerful white minority, it speaks to our own reluctance to get involved: 'Let me not be afraid to defend . . .' Upsetting the status quo is costly. Justice comes at a price.

Alan Paton was sometimes criticized for not advocating a more radical, single-minded approach to ending apartheid, but, like St Paul before him, he recognized the importance of faith, hope and (the greatest of all) love. Loving our neighbour means being Christ's eyes and ears on earth, his hands and feet also. Being the body of Christ challenges us 'to do some work of peace' this coming day.

Can we make this prayer our own in the fight against global poverty? Hearing the cries of the poor, can we add our voice to those seeking an end to unpayable debts, unfair trade rules and insufficient aid, and help to make poverty history? Without justice, there can be no peace.

Annabel Shilson-Thomas

A Song of Anselm

Jesus, like a mother you gather your people to you;
you are gentle with us as a mother with her children.

Often you weep over our sins and our pride,
tenderly you draw us from hatred and judgement.

You comfort us in sorrow and bind up our wounds,
in sickness you nurse us, and with pure milk you feed us.

Jesus, by your dying we are born to new life;
by your anguish and labour we come forth in joy.

Despair turns to hope through your sweet goodness;
through your gentleness we find comfort in fear.

Your warmth gives life to the dead,
your touch makes sinners righteous.

Lord Jesus, in your mercy heal us;
in your love and tenderness remake us.

In your compassion bring grace and forgiveness,
For the beauty of heaven may your love prepare us.

St Anselm (1033–1109), from *Common Worship: Daily Prayer*

It is always difficult to lead the prayers of others when you feel angry about something. It's too easy to hijack public intercessions with barely concealed opinion. Along with many others, I suspect, I felt this acutely at the outbreak of the war in Iraq in March 2003.

While my visceral revulsion at the war grew, I sensed my ability to make space for others' prayers diminishing. At such times, I look for ways of praying that are oblique, evocative, perhaps echoing something of the current crisis, but not too directly.

I hope that we can each be nudged into prayer in different ways, and no one is railroaded by my personal agenda. I, too, am allowed space to pray and feel that my passions are heard by God. Preparing to lead prayers for peace, I was grateful to stumble across the Song of Anselm in *Common Worship: Daily Prayer* (Church House Publishing, 2005, page 639). It is a distillation of the poetic passions expressed in his work, in particular the 'Prayer to St Paul' (in *Prayers and Meditations of Saint Anselm*, Penguin Classics, 1973).

Enriching the Christian Year (SPCK, 1993) wisely suggests the prayer or song be used for Mothering Sunday, and I found its insistent yet un-postured feminine imagery touched me while massive, expensive military might was wielded and a wickedly manipulative man's statue was pulled down. As I perceived bullies bullying a bully, I found Anselm's calm demeanour displacing the anger.

As fake moral authority was being claimed by people on both sides of the conflict, I was drawn to the prayers of a man who felt unworthy to hold the office of Archbishop of Canterbury, but who then instinctively held it in such a way as to command real authority (like some of his modern successors). While political and media machines worked so hard to persuade, and bombs generated so much fear, Anselm's description of Christ 'gathering' and 'tenderly drawing us' away from violence and pride rang with wisdom.

Just when the prayer might seem too soft, too cosy, the anguish of childbirth firmly but gently puts male notions of strength in their place. Again, just as words like 'sweet goodness' might have seemed naive, the phrase 'your warmth gives life to the dead' awakened the spine-tingling memory that the creative power of God, which made the world, also quietly raised Jesus from the dead. This is the gentle, awesome power that commands authority over human fears and ideologies.

This canticle captures the gentle, strong prayer of a man who knew harsh rejection from his bereaved father and who stood up to the manipulative behaviour of a greedy king, but without losing his gracious touch. Anselm was exiled from England for resisting William Rufus's money-grabbing efforts to control the Church, but still refused to play his monarch's competitive game. He had the moral astuteness to see that the office of the Crown was bigger than the fickle man who wore it, and so he could find the grace to ask the Pope to tone down his condemnation of William. That part of Anselm's story rebuked me, and opened the way for me to pray for our leaders and for Saddam Hussein more graciously.

The week in which war broke out, our church said goodbye to an old airman. We remembered his gruelling experience in the Second World War, especially as a prisoner of war. Going to war again as he died, we wondered with heavy hearts whether our generation had proved worthy of his sacrifice. But his gentle, gracious demeanour did at least give us all hope that, after ugly conflict, beauty may return. In the turmoil of war, he gave us a hint that the beauty of heaven was still, is still, worth looking for.

David Warbrick

A vision

O God, our Heavenly Father,
give us a vision of our world
as your love would make it:
A world where the weak are protected
and none go hungry or poor;
A world where the benefits of civilized life are shared,
and everyone can enjoy them;
A world where different races, nations
and cultures live in tolerance
and mutual respect;
A world where peace is built with justice,
and justice is guided by love;
And give us the inspiration and courage to build it,
through Jesus Christ our Lord. Amen.

St Martin-in-the-Fields

When we said we would be moving to Trafalgar Square, one of the confirmation group on the Isle of Dogs went to check it out for us. She came back worried: 'You won't like it,' she said. 'It's all tourists. There's no community there.'

We were moving from a place surrounded by the River Thames and the West India Docks, in which 98 per cent of the electoral roll lived in the parish, to the parish which, as they almost say in the lager advertisement, is probably the most open in the world. Visitors from overseas make up about half the worshippers at St Martin-in-the-Fields on any Sunday. They give us a privileged window into the worldwide, and not just Anglican, Church. We even have a midday 'Visitors to London' service. This prayer was written for that service in 1987 by Canon Geoffrey Brown, the Vicar, with help from the Revd John Pridmore, now the Rector of Hackney and *Church Times* diarist, but then with oversight of St Martin's international ministry. It has become one of the best-loved of our prayers, used on the BBC World Service, set to music by a church in the United States, and even printed on the Christmas cards sent last year by the lawyer of the band REM.

Iris Murdoch wrote an essay titled 'Vision and Choice in Morality'.

Vision is what gives us a sense of other possible worlds. It makes us restless with what is unsatisfactory in the here and now. Jesus' vision of the kingdom of God is what we Christians are restless for. We pray every day, as Christ taught, for God's kingdom to come on earth as in heaven.

This prayer for the world might be a commentary on that phrase of the Lord's Prayer. It is a civilized and civilizing prayer for the common good, recognizing duties and responsibilities for the poor, and a longing for the best of what it is to be human. It is an expression of the conviction that we exist only in community.

In 1914, the Revd Dick Sheppard's vision for St Martin's was of all sorts of people coming in and finding their home. It is the royal parish church and the parish church of those who are homeless and who gravitate to the centre of our capital city either to get lost or to be found. In this, St Martin's is like every parish church, only perhaps more so: a big, broad, inclusive community.

I am repeatedly struck by how deep is the longing for community and for a better and more loving world. It is even more encouraging when people show their willingness to do something about it. Every year there is a nothing-short-of-miraculous St Martin's Christmas Appeal on BBC Radio 4. It has been an annual event since 1927, thanks to Lord Reith and the BBC's continuing generosity. It funds our work with homeless people and those in need all over the country. In 2004 it raised in excess of £600,000. Every year my hope is that people will continue to put their money where their prayer is. If they don't, there is more than a funding gap.

Nicholas Holtam

Down to earth

When we stand gazing upwards, bring us down to earth:
   with the love of a friend
   through the songs of the sorrowing
   in the faces of the hungry.

When we look to you for action, demand some work of us
   by your touch of fire
   your glance of reproof
   your fearful longing.

As ruler over all:
   love us into action;
   fire us with your zeal;
   enrich us with your grace
   to make us willing subjects of your rule.

Janet Nightingale, Christian Aid, from Acts 1–2

This prayer comes from my well-thumbed copy of *Bread of Tomorrow*, a collection of prayers edited by Janet Morley, subtitled 'Praying with the world's poor' (SPCK, 1992, 2004). The prayer takes its inspiration from the disciples gazing up at the ascended Christ. It is a call to active discipleship, a reminder that the gospel is something to be lived out.

The prayer appeals to me because it speaks to my experience that God is often found when I am actively involved in caring for others. I am not a natural contemplative, and have at times undervalued my own spirituality because it seems more earthbound than heavenly. It is in the moments when I feel present for others as someone who knows the love of God and longs to share it that I feel a heightened sense of God's presence. This prayer reminds us that being down to earth is an important part of living out our Christian life, and that we find God speaking to us through 'the love of a friend, the songs of the sorrowing, the faces of the hungry'.

The prayer is written in the context of the world's poor, and I am well aware that, beyond watching the news, I have little experience of those who live in poverty. Yet my years in the ministry have brought me in touch with many who are sorrowing, and others who, though materially comfortable, are hungry for love and a purpose for their lives. In these various encounters, I have found the presence of God. And as the prayer says, God has demanded work from me.

This prayer seems to me a call for us to be compassionate – literally to feel with others and to do so because we are aware of the deep compassion of God. Out of deep love for the world, Jesus Christ lived and served, died and rose again. We are now his body on earth, and it is through our actions that God's compassionate love can reach our fellow human beings. We are reminded that God expects much of us. The 'glance of reproof' and 'fearful longing' convey God's hope that we will live up to expectations.

Yet God's expectations come with God's ability to equip us. We will be loved into action, inspired with zeal, and enriched with grace. God's desire is that we may truly be the body of Christ ministering here. The prayer is a request that God will help us to see others with compassion – that we may be loved, inspired and equipped so that we may act out the faith we proclaim.

Emma Percy

Truth in my heart

That truth has been inscribed into my heart
　　and into the heart of every human being,
there to be read and reverenced,
thanks be to you, O God.
That there are ways of seeing
　　and sensitivities of knowing
hidden deep in the palace of the soul,
waiting to be discovered,
ready to be set free,
thanks be to you.
Open my senses to wisdom's inner promptings
that I may give voice to what I hear in my soul
and be changed for the healing of the world,
that I may listen for truth in every living soul
and be changed for the well-being of the world.

J. Philip Newell, from *Sounds of the Eternal*

Sometimes our religious traditions have given us the impression that wisdom is essentially foreign to us. Too often, it has been assumed that truth is like an external deposit, watched over by our teaching authorities, and that it will be dispensed to us like medication from a pharmacist. Yet Ecclesiasticus says that wisdom was born with us in the womb (Ecclesiasticus 1.14). Similarly, St Paul says that truth has been inscribed in our inner being (Romans 2.15).

We may have become distant from it, and it may have become distorted within, but it is there, waiting to be recovered in our lives and relationships. In part, prayer is about listening attentively to what God has etched into the core of our being. This prayer in particular is about thankfulness for the inner text of our heart and the belief that we can read it, not simply for ourselves, but for the healing of the world.

Early in our British Christian tradition, a Welsh monk was asked by a young woman for a rule of life. She was considering a contemplative vocation, and wanted him to tell her how to live. 'Don't ask me,' he said. 'What has God written on your heart? Learn to read there what God has etched into your being. When you have read your inner text, write it out on a piece of parchment and allow that to become your rule of life. But once you have written out what you have read within, compare what you have written with the perfect expression, the Word made flesh. And if there is discord between what you have read in your heart and what is uttered in Christ, know that you have misread your heart, and go back and read again.'

This is an important story, for at least two reasons. First, it affirms that truth has been written into the core of our being and into the heart of every human, and that it is imperative to read that text. No one else can do that for us. It is not for the spiritual teacher to replace our inner text with another, but to help us read our inner being.

Second, the story emphasizes that we are not left to our own subjectivity. Christ is the measuring rod for our inner explorations. It is not, however, a foreign truth that Christ embodies. Yes, we may have become foreign to our own depths, but Christ shows us the deepest inscriptions of our souls. He shows us the truth that is deeper than the falseness of what we have done or become in our lives. It is a truth that will set us free, not to become something other than ourselves, but to become truly ourselves. Above all, it sets us free to give ourselves away to one another in love, for that is the greatest wisdom.

'Open my senses to wisdom's inner promptings that I may give voice to what I hear in my soul and be changed for the healing of the world.'

J. Philip Newell

The fountain of all wisdom

I implore you, good Jesus,
that as in your mercy you have given me
to drink in with delight the words of your knowledge,
so of your loving kindness
you will also grant me one day to come to you,
the fountain of all wisdom,
and to stand for ever before your face.
Amen.

The Venerable Bede (673–735)

This prayer stands at the foot of the Venerable Bede's grave in Durham Cathedral. I became familiar with it as an ordinand in Durham. So long as I had a couple of minutes to spare, I could pay homage to Bede on my way to lectures, with a detour around the cathedral cloisters and through the glorious Galilee Chapel where he is buried.

Here was inspiration for any student: someone who saw the values of learning, yet apparently kept perspective. Certainly this prayer helped me to find the person amid a pile of books, and a drink in (what occasionally feels like) the desert of academe. The goal of learning is not graduation, nor ordination. The goal of learning is wisdom; and wisdom grows as we seek the face of Christ.

Wisdom, I suspect, is not near the top of many people's wish-lists. In a world of talk-show celebrities and instant credit, where does it fit? It's hard to relate to Solomon, who chose wisdom (most, given a choice, would opt for wealth); or to St Paul, who prayed that the Church be filled with knowledge of God, when perhaps many would ask that the Church be filled with a good number of reliable folk who covenant.

The scriptures persistently urge us to seek wisdom above wealth. Indeed, wisdom is one of the few commodities we are specifically instructed to ask for: 'If any of you is lacking in wisdom,' writes James, 'ask God, who gives to all, generously and ungrudgingly' (James 1.5).

Wisdom doesn't appeal. We've forgotten that, to the Hebrew mind, wisdom was eminently practical, helping the wise to distinguish between right and wrong, and to follow God's path. We have more often pulled our images of wisdom from Greek thought, in which we encounter an otherworldly sage contemplating the mysteries, or a clever debater arguing the finer points with verbal agility. So we pursue degrees, yet still pine for wisdom.

Bede expresses Christologically the chorus that resounds through the book of Proverbs: the fear of the Lord is the beginning of wisdom. Wisdom begins with our recognition of our need, with our longing for God, with our hunger for growth. Our predecessors set about wisdom as if it were a matter of life and death.

Insofar as Bede found wisdom, he found it not so much through ecclesiastical history as through prayer. I suspect the ancients may have been better at acknowledging God as the source of all wisdom than modern believers can manage, prone as we are to deny the limits of human understanding. 'Though I do not know myself,' prayed Hilary, a fourth-century Christian, 'yet I perceive so much that I marvel at thee the more because I am ignorant of myself.' We praise the source of faith and learning, not only because God deserves our adoration, but also because it preserves us from intellectual arrogance and self-pride.

Every year at Epiphany we contemplate the 'wise men' who willingly travelled afar in search of wisdom. Clearly these people took wisdom seriously: they watched the stars; they experienced other cultures; perhaps they read avidly. But their journey was fulfilled, their hunger satisfied, when they reached Bethlehem: when they came to Christ, the source of all wisdom, and stood before his face.

Jo Bailey Wells

Enlighten our minds

O Lord, heavenly Father, in whom is the fullness of light and wisdom, enlighten our minds by thy Holy Spirit and give us grace to receive thy word with reverence and humility, without which no man can understand thy truth, for Christ's sake.

John Calvin (1509–64)

Most Bible studies begin with a prayer. But how many could truly be described as an act of prayer – the collective reading of scripture as an act of communion with God?

The word 'study' is probably unhelpful, as it makes us feel that we should be looking at the blackboard or reading learned commentaries. It simultaneously de-skills us, while convincing us that reading the Bible is an enterprise that we have to work hard at. No wonder most Christians neglect it.

Calvin's prayer, however, suggests an approach in which God plays a more central part. For Calvin, reading scripture was a Spirit-guided activity. Unless we approach it with reverence and humility, and with the enlightenment of the Holy Spirit, reading the Bible will be a fruitless exercise: 'The word will not find acceptance in men's hearts before it is sealed by the inward testimony of the Spirit' (Institutes I.7.4).

Despite his emphasis on the clarity and literal sense of the Bible, Calvin did not crudely equate the words of scripture with the word of God. The word can speak to us only when the Spirit authenticates the witness of the biblical authors in our own hearts. This contrasts starkly with later theories of the verbal inerrancy of scripture, in which the Holy Spirit seems to be less the Comforter than the 'Enforcer', beating down our scepticism and intellectual freedom.

This prayer asks that, by the power of the Spirit, the voice of the scriptures might enter into our frustrated attempts to understand. If we become tempted to restrict our reading to the 'words' of scripture, it is the Spirit that leads us beyond the words to the Word of God, turning the reading into an encounter with Christ. That is why all Bible study must begin with an invocation of the Spirit. Just as the breaking of the bread in the eucharist comes after the *epiclesis*, so must the breaking of the word. As St Ephrem said: 'Only when we are filled with the Spirit can we drink in Christ.'

So Bible study can be a eucharistic action: a process of receiving from

God in response to our own intellectual offering. And, just as holy communion is the sacrament of the unity of the Church, so perhaps Calvin's prayer might point to a way of reading the Bible that could unite rather than divide us.

Beginning from humility and reverence, rather than entrenched positions, we must pray for the Spirit to lead us into the truth of the scriptures. On the road to Emmaus, it was necessary for the risen Jesus to explain the scriptures to the disciples – the Word interpreted the words. And it was in the breaking of the bread that this hermeneutic was completed: Christ's identity was disclosed and faith was born.

It is the Holy Spirit that enables this *lectio divina* (inspired reading) in the Church today. So, as we study the scriptures, we pray, with Calvin, that the Spirit of truth and unity will lead us into the fullness of wisdom.

James Walters

The voice of the victims

Hear our voice,
for it is the voice of the victims of all wars
  and violence among individuals and nations.
Hear our voice,
for it is the voice of all children who suffer and will suffer
  when people put their trust in weapons and war.
Hear our voice,
when we beg you to instil into the hearts of all human beings
  the wisdom of peace, the strength of justice
and the joy of fellowship . . .
O God, hear our voice
and grant unto the world your everlasting peace.

Pope John Paul II (1920–2005) at Hiroshima, 25 February 1981

We live in the age of the soundbite. Amid the cacophony of voices that we hear in our globalized and media-saturated world, getting your voice heard today requires a clear message and maximum exposure. You can no longer rely on the power of your argument or the importance of your message. Today 'the medium is the message', and communication is big business. No wonder, then, that the voices that shape our day-to-day reality are predominantly those of well-funded political leaders, big corporations, and overpaid celebrities.

This prayer of Pope John Paul II, however, tells us that being a Christian is about rejecting this competitive business of getting your voice heard. On the contrary, our voice should not be our own at all. The voice of the Church is the voice of the voiceless. Just as Jesus was silent in front of Pontius Pilate, so the Church of Christ stands in solidarity with those who continue to be silenced by the violence of power and the suffering of war.

Nobody in human history has been silenced as quickly and brutally as the 140,000 people who perished in Hiroshima and Nagasaki in 1945. The Pope's visit to that site of nuclear holocaust in 1981, for which this prayer was written, did much to draw the attention of Christians to its singular importance. Never before had the potential for the rapid large-scale destruction of humanity been realized. It was the advent of the 'culture of death', as John Paul famously characterized our modern world.

We seem to have learned little from the past. As John Paul went on to say: 'To remember the past is to commit oneself to the future. To remember Hiroshima is to abhor nuclear war. To remember Hiroshima is to commit oneself to peace.'

Whether or not Christians can accept that there was a historical necessity for nuclear deterrence, this prayer calls us to question how comfortably the Church can live today with this large-scale potential for human destruction. It suggests that we cannot pray for the kingdom while putting our trust in weapons and war. Rather, we must pray for the wisdom of peace built, not through fear of annihilation, but through the strength of justice.

And that is a prayer we make, not with our own voices, but with the voices of those who have already been silenced, and those who continue to be silenced in wars today. Theirs is the only credible voice with which we can speak to God for our world.

James Walters

Peace

Prayer for the Nations

O God,
who wouldest fold both heaven and earth in a single peace:
Let the design of thy great love
lighten upon the waste of our wraths and sorrows;
and give peace to thy Church,
peace among nations,
peace in our dwellings,
and peace in our hearts;
through thy Son our Saviour,
Jesus Christ.
Amen.

Eric Milner-White (1884–1963), Dean of York Minster

These words resonate in my mind from the days when I was a chorister. But I was recently given a handwritten version of them that struck even deeper chords.

The prayer first appeared in Eric Milner-White's *Memorials upon Several Occasions* in 1933, and he subsequently included it in his anthology *Daily Prayer*, first published in 1941. Milner-White had been a chaplain on the Western Front in the First World War.

I remember the prayer being used by David Stewart-Smith, a musically and spiritually gifted priest who, like Milner-White, had also been on the staff of King's College, Cambridge, and York Minster. It was David's widow Kathleen who shortly after his death gave me a copy of it in his handwriting, and asked me to continue to pray these words for the peace of the nations.

David's remarkable ministry was distinguished by many events and accomplishments, but two international conflicts darkened its background. The greater of them was the Second World War, but the other was the chilling initiation in 1967 of conflict in the Holy Land, where David had worked at St George's Cathedral in Jerusalem. The connection between the sombre shadows of conflict and bloodshed, the use of this prayer in public worship, and my own boyhood recollections of evensong, is music.

It is not an arbitrary connection. In the use of music as prayer, the horror of conflict and the longing for reconciliation can find powerful expression. The psychologist Anthony Storr suggests, in *Music and the Mind*, that music has a restorative capacity that can lead to reconciling our inner conflicts and the recovery of wholeness.

Music is an ancient vehicle for the expression in worship of shared desire. The songs at the core of the Church's daily worship are the psalms, in which music – songs – feature prominently. Psalm 139, a song about not being able to sing, is a haunting account of that wasteland of wrath and sorrow which is exile from homeland: 'How shall we sing the Lord's song in a strange land?' For worship in the temple in Jerusalem had taught songs that highlighted the expectation of peace and prosperity: 'Peace be within thy walls and plenteousness within thy palaces' (Psalm 122).

The temple songs of Jerusalem are an expression of belief that worship on earth opens us up to experience that is configured with the eternal life of God in heaven, where music is a consistent metaphor for harmony and peace. Thus the song of the living creatures in Isaiah's vision is echoed not only in the end-time revelation to John, but also in our worship in the eucharist. It is here, pre-eminently, that we anticipate the configuring of earth with heaven; here that the gifts of unity and peace, sealed in communion, are heralded by that song of eternity, 'Holy, Holy, Holy, Lord God Almighty, which was and is and is to come' (Revelation 4.8).

An appreciation of the potential of music shapes our hope for the fulfilment of this prayer in a scriptural vision of peace. In the words of a song from a very different context, 'I'd like to teach the world to sing, in perfect harmony . . .'

Martin Warner

A prayer for unity

O God, the Father of our Lord Jesus Christ,
our only Saviour, the Prince of Peace;
Give us grace seriously to lay to heart
the great dangers we are in by our unhappy divisions.
Take away all hatred and prejudice,
and whatever else may hinder us
from godly union and concord;
that, as there is but one Body, and one Spirit,
and one hope of our calling,
one Lord, one faith, one baptism,
one God and Father of us all,
so we may henceforth be all of one heart,
and of one soul, united in one holy bond
of truth and peace, of faith and charity,
and may with one mind and one mouth
glorify thee; through Jesus Christ our Lord. Amen.

From the Accession service in the
Book of Common Prayer (1703)

So far, I've never been to an Accession service, the only one of the state services to survive in the present form of the Book of Common Prayer. There used to be other state services, including one to commemorate the great fire of London; St Paul's Cathedral continued to hold that service until 1859, and gave it up only when the holiday that accompanied it was scrapped by Parliament.

Forms of prayer to commemorate the gunpowder plot (5 November), the beheading of Charles I (30 January) and the restoration of Charles II (29 May) may now seem to belong to an arcane region of liturgical history, and I would doubt that the Liturgical Commission is considering revisions for contemporary use. But the significance of these national days of prayer, accompanied by holidays, seems to have given the Church of England an important role historically in articulating some sense of a shared identity and spirituality.

In 1703, the Accession service was revised into its present form for Queen Anne, and the prayer for unity was added then. As a new century began, the division and turmoil of the seventeenth century still scarred social, political and religious life in England. Anti-Catholic paranoia had jostled with ruthless suppression of Puritanism; sleaze had tinged every new beginning at the Court. Even as godly a priest as Henry Sacheverell could with confidence 'hang out a bloody banner of defiance' in a sermon in St Paul's that condemned the toleration of Dissenters in 1709.

In contrast with these familiar themes, which we cannot with any air of superiority identify as characteristic only of the past, the gift of a day's holiday provided a moment for reflection, in which the whole nation was called 'seriously to lay to heart the great dangers we are in by our unhappy divisions'. Today, if we might be permitted to pause and reflect, the words of this prayer call Christians to a recovery of unity, 'one Lord, one faith, one baptism', that can only be given to those from whose hearts hatred and prejudice have been banished by the giver of unity, the Holy Spirit.

But the location of this prayer in one of the state services indicates that the gift of unity, if we are able to receive it, is not simply a spiritual ornament. With its echoes of all the vicissitudes of our history, the use of this prayer today calls the Church to look beyond itself for the context in which it is itself called to be a force for unity in contemporary society.

Being a force for unity requires the Church to be a sign that consistently calls prejudice into question; that confidently unmasks hypocrisy wherever it is to be found; and that joyfully defends human dignity as an essential condition for the recognition of God as creator. Only so may we with one mind and one mouth give glory to that same God, and claim to live as citizens of the kingdom of the Prince of Peace.

Martin Warner

I am two men

I am two men;
and one is longing to serve thee utterly, and one is afraid.
O Lord, have compassion upon me.
I am two men;
and one will labour to the end, and one is already weary.
O Lord, have compassion upon me.
I am two men;
and one knows the suffering of the world, and one knows only his own.
O Lord, have compassion upon me.
And may the Spirit of our Lord Jesus Christ
Fill my heart and the hearts of all men everywhere.

Used by Prebendary Austen Williams (1912–2001)

A few years ago, I took the funeral of a man who had been homeless for more than 30 years. He was a well known and much loved character. After a morning in St Martin-in-the-Fields, he would walk down to Parliament and sit in the central lobby of the House of Commons. Consequently, his funeral was attended by an astonishing number of people, including many parliamentarians.

Tony Benn gave an address: 'Mr Andrews sat in Parliament for over 30 years. Unlike most MPs, he never lost his seat.' I invited everyone to put a flower in a vase in memory of Robert, and, if they wanted, to say something about him. Thus 60 or so people pieced together this man's fragmented and complex life, which each of us knew only in part. Perhaps that is how it is with most of us.

I think this prayer was written by Prebendary Austen Williams, Vicar of St Martin-in-the-Fields from 1956 to 1984, the longest-serving of my twentieth-century predecessors. Certainly he used the prayer in countless broadcasts, but I have never seen it attributed to him. When I asked him directly if he wrote it, he said, 'I am not sure,' and then talked about the way everything has more than one origin.

He also said that it was unusable now because the meaning of language has changed. So I think he gave us permission to pray, 'I am two people', though that is nothing like as elegant. Use of this prayer always evokes requests for copies. It catches something about our nature that we know to be true.

St Martin, that great saint, was Bishop of Tours from 372 until his death in 397. If not exactly two men, there were two very distinct aspects to his life. As a soldier, he longed to be baptized, but this could happen only after he had done his full length of service in the Roman army.

His life was deeply paradoxical. Having been baptized and ordained deacon by Hilary of Poitiers, he lived as a hermit, but attracted a community of about 70 around him. He was a reluctant Bishop of Tours, who so hated life in the city that he moved out to the caves beside the Loire.

On Sundays, he would go into the city to pray with the *energoumenoi*, the outcasts who were often mentally ill and dispossessed, and bless oil for the faithful to take away in flasks to anoint the sick. He is a tremendous patron saint for our city-centre church 'in the fields' and with a ministry to people no one else wants.

Given Martin's life, it is not surprising that he became the patron saint of both soldiers and pacifists. Coincidentally, St Martin-in-the-Fields is the parish church of the Admiralty and the Ministry of Defence as well as the church most associated with the founding of the Peace Pledge Union by the Revd Dick Sheppard, another former Vicar. In the past 20 years, there has been a remarkable convergence in the practical implications of the just war and pacifist traditions of Christian ethics. There are wider lessons here about how the Church can live creatively with moral diversity.

So, 'I am two men' feels right descriptively: that's how I am. It is also right in terms of what we long for. Jesus taught us to be honest before God, and to pray for what we want. This prayer does both these things, acknowledging our need for God's mercy, and voicing our longing to be the people God would have us be.

Nicholas Holtam

Universal prayer for peace

Lead me from death to life,
from falsehood to truth.
Lead me from despair to hope,
from fear to trust.
Lead me from hate to love,
from war to peace.
Let peace fill our heart,
our world, our universe.

Anonymous

When the Franciscans moved into Whitechapel in the early 1980s, they introduced themselves to their neighbours. The news that they prayed four times a day was met with blank incomprehension by the white East-enders on one side, but the Bengali Muslims on the other side said: 'Ah, that's like us. We pray five times a day.'

London is 'a world city' in religious terms, as well as culturally, eco-nomically and politically. The lively presence of other faiths has awakened a wider interest in religion. Once again, faith matters. In a world in which religion fuels some of the great conflicts, the question of how we can pray together is pressing, particularly how we can pray for peace.

Gandhi was a universalist who had a profound regard for Jesus and for the world's other great moral and religious teachers. There was a marvellous exchange in the film *Gandhi* when the Revd C. F. Andrews, a remarkable Christian missionary, and Gandhi were pushed into the gutter by two South African Boers. Gandhi asked the meaning of Jesus' teaching that we should 'turn the other cheek'. When Andrews said that Jesus was speaking metaphorically, Gandhi replied: 'No, I think he meant what he said.'

In January 1998, on the 50th anniversary of Gandhi's assassination, the actor Ben Kingsley read from the writings of the Mahatma or 'great soul' in the pulpit of St Martin-in-the-Fields. At the end, he added unex-pectedly: 'When I despair, I remember that all through history, the way of truth and love has always won. There have been tyrants, and, for a time, they have seemed invincible, but, in the end, they always fall. Think of it: always.'

The power of those words sent me off on a pilgrimage to the ashram at Sevagram in the middle of India, where Gandhi lived for 12 years. The prayer-ground is, as Gandhi taught, spacious and open to the sky, a place freely accessible to the poorest of the poor. Early each morning, the prayers of the world's religions were recited in turn.

In that context, the Lord's Prayer rooted me in strange and unfamiliar territory, and made it possible for me to pray some of the other prayers as my own. This universal prayer for peace has Jainist and Hindu origins, as well as this elegant version, which was widely circulated in the 1980s.

There is a fascinating story in the travels of Marco Polo, retold in William Dalrymple's *In Xanadu*. In the Persian city of Saveh, Marco Polo found the tombs of the Magi who went to worship Christ. Their gifts of gold, frankincense and myrrh had their familiar meanings, except that, for Zoroastrians, the myrrh was to show that Christ was a physician.

Dalrymple also remembered an account of the Persian defeat of the Byzantines in the seventh century, in which they swept through Palestine, destroying all the important buildings. The single exception was the Church of the Nativity in Bethlehem, because over the doorway was a huge mosaic of the recognizably Persian Magi bringing gifts to the Christ-child.

In the season of Advent we prepare to celebrate again the birth of the Prince of Peace. Each year St Martin's produces a booklet of Advent meditations, and the theme of one of these concentrated on the idea of seeds, germination, nurture and growth, rich in the possibilities of waiting with expectation, as well as the need for compost. What are the seeds laid down in his life that will help us to pray for the peace of the world? Could we use this universal prayer for peace to help us find common ground with those who see God differently?

Nicholas Holtam

Darkness and sin

Hallowed, apparently

Dear Lord. Hallowed be thy name, apparently. Which is a bit worrying. Don't get me wrong, it's nice that you're hallowed and everything, it's just that hallowedness can really get in the way of the warm, smiley, arm-around-the-shoulder type things, and they mean a lot to me. You see, when I meet human beings who are only just ever-so-slightly hallowed, I'm no good with them. I get awkward and dorky, and they start to think I'm a bit odd. I don't want you to think that. I want you to see my jaunty familiarity as a breath of fresh air. However, it's always in the back of my mind that, on the Judgement Day, you might say, 'Not him. I don't feel he ever truly acknowledged my hallowedness,' and I'd be dragged off, calling back to you that your hallowedness was so fundamental and profound that I'd felt there was no need to up-front it. And some of the more liberal angels would deliberately not catch your eye.

Frank Skinner

I haven't prayed this prayer. I read it. By the time Christopher Graham Collins had written it and included it in his autobiography, he was known as the comedian Frank Skinner.

Although his blunt language and unabashed recollections of sexual encounters may prevent some from enjoying his company, I hope I'm not being merely contrary in finding his prayer worth reflection. If I relate one striking anecdote, you might understand why I feel his prayers have gravity and compel me to think about who is near to God.

Skinner gives a devastatingly bleak account of his encounter with a prostitute. Shockingly, but not gratuitously, he conveys the woman's deep loneliness, and suggests a vast hinterland of sadness. He evokes the desperate shallowness of the sex and his own pathos. As he leaves her, he says, 'It's been a business doing pleasure with you,' and I'm not sure whether to laugh or cry. His humorous observation is unstoppable, consistent and painfully searching.

It is unquestionably the same man – extravagant, incisive, successful, foolish, quizzical and passionate – who speaks to God in his autobiography in seven prayers, which, he says, 'give you a fair idea of what my relationship with God is like'.

Most of them involve teasing questions, like the delightful one about typos in the Bible. (What if it was the 'matted calf', he asks, reminding the prodigal son of the consequences of his neglect of the cattle.) They make me want to answer the questions and explain things, as with his superb prayer challenging God about the possibility of hell. But I know he'd always be two steps ahead in the conversation, and would soon be sending up my over-professional, self-justifying need to answer.

These prayers, in the context of his story, reveal someone whose frankness with God always resolves with a touching acceptance that there need not be a rounded ending. This comedian knows that greater depth of relationship is found in teasing questions, going to and fro, than in the fleeting satisfaction of clear-cut answers.

Of all the prayers, this one evokes most sympathy. When he says, touchingly, that he's 'awkward and dorky' with 'ever-so-slightly hallowed' people, I have a sense of how he feels. There is, however, a slight tease in Skinner's use of the word 'hallowedness', conveying his awe, while hinting at the possibility of God's self-importance.

Then a beautifully made plea: surely it was precisely God's deep hallowedness that should banish pretentious piety. Liberal angels avert their gaze, embarrassed by God's judgement. Again, I'm not sure whether to laugh or cry. I wonder how church makes people feel. How tragic if our well-intentioned pious demeanour accidentally leaves some awkwardly wondering whether God thinks they're clumsy or odd, when in fact they may be closer to him than we are.

This 'what if?' prayer begins as though it might be a bland plea for mateyness with God, but ends with surprising subtlety. It does pose questions for both God and Frank Skinner, but it is more about exposing feeling than expecting an answer.

At the beginning, the comedian seems far from God, but in the end, as the embarrassed angels know, he is very close. Frank's comic astuteness, his accepting faith and eye for vivid detail and contradiction, observing God and self and prostitute with equal candour, must surely make him refreshing company for a God who loves truth.

David Warbrick

Veronica

Gentle Father of our Lord Jesus Christ,
and Lord of all consolation:
Give us, after the example of blessed Veronica,
to bind up the wounded and to care for the sorrowful;
that, in us, Christ may be awakened
   and the beauty of his face be revealed;
who died and rose again for us,
and lives and reigns, one God,
   for ever and ever. Amen.

David Silk

I was once challenged about kneeling to kiss the star on the floor of the underground chapel in the Church of the Nativity in Bethlehem: 'How do you know that Jesus was born right here – on this very spot?'

I had to reply: 'It just doesn't matter.' And it doesn't matter to me whether or not Veronica actually existed.

She is a shadowy figure, with what is literally a walk-on part in the Passion of our Lord. She does not even have a name. 'Veronica' we call her, for that simply means 'a true image'. She is said to have wiped the blood and sweat from the face of Jesus as he made his way to Calvary. As a reward, there was left on her handkerchief an image of his features.

While the story may or may not be historically true, it does enshrine a profound spiritual truth. Veronica loves kindness and mercy (Micah 6.8). By showing them, the character of Christ is imprinted on her life. St Paul has this in mind when he writes:

Blessed be the God and Father of our Lord Jesus Christ, a gentle Father and the Lord of all consolation, who comforts us in all our sorrows, so that we can offer to others, in their sorrows, the consolation we have received from God ourselves. Indeed, as the sufferings of Christ overflow to us, so through Christ does our consolation overflow. (2 Corinthians 1.2–5)

At home, when eyes fill up with tears; at work, when tensions rise; in slums, when rats rake through dustbins; in courts, when accusations and exaggerations replace discussions; in hospitals, when the doctors are unable to offer more than pain relief – the face of Christ is there for blood and tears and sweat to be wiped away. By kindness and mercy, consolation is given, and the image of Christ is indelibly imprinted on the life of the giver.

If we would be like Jesus, we must act like him. When we act like him, we begin to resemble him. Strange though it is, when we discipline ourselves to act kindly, even at times when we do not feel like it, we find that we really do feel like it. Being generous to an enemy can help to make us generous. It is the mystery of how giving love can elicit love, even from the hardest heart.

Another way of entering into the mystery is the metaphor of 'dressing up in Christ' (Colossians 3.9–10). In baptism, we 'put on Christ', as we don the baptismal white robe of renewed innocence. The grace of the sacrament means that what we are deemed to be, we actually become. In the old language of bygone debates, 'imputed' righteousness becomes 'imparted' righteousness.

St John of the Cross writes of this in *The Living Flame of Love*. Christ is planted in us by the grace of baptism and confirmation. So our growth in Christian living may be expressed as an awakening of the presence of Christ within us, the revealing of his face in our lives.

As St Paul puts it: 'Just as we have borne the image of the man of dust, so shall we bear the image of the man of heaven' (1 Corinthians 15.49). A kind deed is the melody that tunes our ear to the music of heaven.

David Silk

Father, forgive

Father, forgive them; for they know not what they do.

Luke 23.34

For a Roman soldier, crucifying people – foreigners, slaves, criminals – was a routine chore. He was unlikely to make a production of it, though we are sadly aware that armies of all ages and nations contain the occasional sadist.

Yet, by and large, the men who had execution duty, as opposed to patrol duty or latrine duty, must have blocked their mind to what was actually involved, and what it would have felt like if it were they who were the unfortunates to be crucified. They merely set themselves the task of doing the job efficiently. Never in their wildest dreams could they have thought that the quiet peasant they nailed up that spring morning was the Son of God.

In a way, the specifics of their 'not knowing' are unimportant. In his parable of the sheep and the goats, Jesus makes the point sharply: what we do to anybody, a 'least brother', we do to him. Our horrified plea that we did not know it was he whom we turned away – unfed, unclothed, sick and lonely – holds no water. Everybody is Jesus; everybody matters.

But this prayer – words said by Jesus himself, the Incarnate Prayer, when he hung on the cross dying – are less about our own refusal to see that everybody is entitled to the same reverence that we feel for God himself, than with our shameful readiness to judge. If we are speaking of sin, then surely the execution, by torture, of our Saviour is the greatest collective sin of humankind.

God came to us in love, and we rejected him. Yet Jesus himself refuses to see this action as a sin. He tells us explicitly: what is being done is through ignorance – they know not what they do – and he asks his father to forgive.

If Jesus sees what was done on Calvary as pitiful rather than wicked, what of the things we see done all around us? What of the crimes, the cruelties, the cheating and lying, the infidelities, the betrayals, the countless sorrowful ways in which we treat each other without reverence? On all sides, in private and in public, do we not see people being made use of, one person or one group subordinating the good of another for a private end?

Sinful, we think or say: evil, hateful to God and to right-thinking humanity. The acts, yes indeed, hateful – but the actors? The man who sexually abuses a small child, the woman who destroys a reputation with her lies, the abusive prison guards: evil? Or, with Jesus, must we not rather say: 'they know not what they do'?

Condemning and even punishing the deed should not involve passing judgement on the doer. That is God's prerogative. Sin is a mysterious affair. We must know what we are doing is wrong, and then choose deliberately to do it. In a terrible way, we need a certain maturity to sin (and maturity is rare). Who are we to tell the clarity in a criminal's mind, the true freedom of a criminal's will, that could make him or her pass from the wretched muddle in which so many of us live into the absoluteness of sin? God knows, and it was well said by St Thérèse of Lisieux, that we should trust as much to his justice as to his mercy.

God knows the genetic equipment with which we each started on our journey into life. He knows the traditions of our training and the pressure of our experiences. He and he alone can evaluate how capable we are of mental clarity or of free choice. We can never know this even of ourselves, and so even our self-judgements, whether good or bad, are inadequate. Certainly all other consciences must remain a mystery to us.

This prayer tackles our instinctive need to judge. It is our way of making sense of life, tabulating people, achieving some sort of control. But it is a false instinct. We can and must deal with the effects of actions, but there the judgement must stop.

Sister Wendy Beckett

The fruits of suffering

O Lord, remember not only the men and women of goodwill, but also
those of ill will. But do not remember all the suffering they have inflicted
upon us. Remember the fruits we bought, thanks to this suffering: our
comradeship, our loyalty, our humility, the courage, the generosity, the
greatness of heart which has grown out of this; and, when they come
to judgement, let all the fruits that we have borne be their forgiveness.
Amen.

Anonymous, Ravensbrück concentration camp

I know a man who was a prisoner of war, forced to work on the Thai
railway under horrific conditions. Ever since – for more than 50 years
– he has searched for the ability to forgive the Japanese soldiers who tortured him. The pain and the longing have virtually crippled him, physically and emotionally. Recently, in his old age, he has reached the point
where he can finally conceive the possibility of forgiving.

Jesus tells us to love our enemies and pray for those who persecute
us (Matthew 5.44; cf. Luke 6.27, 35). That has been the script for my
friend's life ever since the war, even though much of the time it has been
beyond him.

This prayer was found written on a piece of wrapping paper in
Ravensbrück, the largest of the concentration camps for women in Nazi
Germany. We do not know whether it was written by Christians or Jews.
We can only marvel that we, too, through this prayer, are recipients of
the fruits these women bought, 'thanks to' their suffering. On that basis,
I am happy to line up beside the perpetrators and be stretched to great-
ness of heart.

Apart from the grace of God, I do not understand how the transition is
made from the injustice of torture to the freedom of goodwill. In our era,
perhaps it has been demonstrated most visibly by Nelson Mandela – who
would not claim to be a Christian. He invited his white jailer to attend
his presidential inauguration as an honoured guest, the first of many
spectacular gestures he made that showed a breathtaking magnanimity.
President Mandela's willingness to forgive became the inspiration for a
whole nation's reconciliation.

I first came across this prayer in the Chapel of the Holy Innocents
at Norwich Cathedral, and have used it for several years. I am always

struck afresh by the grace it encapsulates. To find the word 'thanks' in the same phrase as suffering is amazing. But it is only recently that I have realized what this prayer does not say. Unlike my PoW friend, these women are not asking God for the ability to forgive those who caused their suffering. Rather, they ask that God might forgive the perpetrators on judgement day.

Perhaps it was too hard for these women to forgive. Certainly, it was less relevant. It seems to me that the women here have moved to a different place. Far from being focused on their own needs, they have become concerned for their abusers. Here is the outworking of Jesus' command to love our enemies and pray for our persecutors. These women are praying for the ultimate welfare of their persecutors on judgement day.

In so doing, they have moved from anger to sadness, and from sadness to hope. Their focus is no longer on their own pain, or even on the evil of those who have hurt them. Like Mandela, their longing is not for retributive justice, but for restorative justice: for courage where there has been fear, for loyalty in place of unfaithfulness, for humility and generosity instead of the abuse of power.

Surely this is the fruit of forgiveness: their suffering has become a resource, a resource from which to minister not only to their captors, but also to the whole of society.

Jo Bailey Wells

Lighten our darkness

Lighten our darkness,
we beseech thee, O Lord;
and by thy great mercy
defend us from all perils and dangers of this night;
for the love of thy only Son, our Saviour Jesus Christ.
Amen.

Third collect at evensong, Book of Common Prayer

This collect is one of the best loved prayers from evensong, and it is also used at compline (see *Common Worship*, page 97). It gives both services a feel of being on the edge: the night is drawing in, but we are enfolded in Christ's love.

Evensong and compline can be said or sung alone or in company, and can seem more accessible than holy communion as a way of sharing worship with those from other Churches. The services are a way for separated members of the universal Church to transcend denominational divisions, and can also help Anglicans to draw together in transcending disagreements within our own family.

Using these forms of prayer engages us in the work of reconciliation that is so badly needed within and between Churches. The anger and hurt that we experience in our conflicts constitute the darkness and the 'perils and dangers' of the Church's 'night'.

The collect is also suitable for Candlemas, a time when Christ is seen as the light of the world. The prayer allows us to see him as one who transforms darkness into light, and so effects salvation. Waiting for such a transformation is like waiting for the fulfilment of a promise, as Simeon realized when he saw the couple approaching him with their baby.

The darkness of the Church, as well as that of the world, is often most palpably real at night, so that, for those of us who have difficulty sleeping, nights can feel long and even frightening. Sleep or morning (whichever comes first) seems like a long-awaited promise. During this period of waiting, which is all the harder because everyone else is asleep, one's perceptions are heightened, so that one is more raw in the face of experience – one's own or that of the world or of the Church.

Memories also become sharper, and this can distort them, allowing them to metamorphose into frightening projections of the future. The hurts of the past, revisited as memories in the lonely hours of the night, become more acute; and there is a temptation to brace oneself for more hurts to come. So night can be a time of fear, in which distrust of others feeds on brooding anxiety.

This can be a prayer to pray slowly in the darkest hours of the night, savouring its capacity to take away fear. It draws us more deeply into God's love, and allows us to acknowledge our painful memories, while easing the way they chafe on our consciousness.

The collect can also be said while holding in mind the world's painful memories, many of which derive from anger and hatred passed from one generation to the next. It allows us to hold the suffering of society in the love of God – its poverty, materialism, broken relationships, and indifference to its need for God.

Sometimes, the late-night news is too vividly present to us. Its stark implications become the 'perils and dangers of this night', and make sleep harder. This short prayer allows us, at such times, to share in the fear in which so many people live. We can be in solidarity with them, so that the waking hours of the night are not wasted.

I have also found that the prayer allows me to experience the darkness of the Church as something in which the seeds of salvation are lying dormant. They are ready to emerge into the light of Christ, which transforms fear into trust. It makes waiting in the dark for sleep or dawn to come a little easier to bear.

Lorraine Cavanagh

Te lucis ante terminum

To you before the end of day,
Creator of the world, we pray:
In love unfailing hear our prayer,
Enfold us in your watchful care.
Keep all disturbing dreams away,
And hold the evil foe at bay.
Repose untroubled let us find
For soul and body, heart and mind.
Almighty Father, this accord
Through Jesus Christ, your Son, our Lord:
Who reigns with you eternally
In your blest Spirit's unity.
Amen.

Anonymous, before 11th century
(translation from St Cecilia's Abbey, Ryde)

Every funeral is sacred, but some surprise us gently with a new insight. As I stood once at a graveside with several hundred mourners from Caribbean islands, I felt humbled, and, dare I say it, elated. There was something remarkable in the air. People were crying, of course; but some were laughing, singing, and filling in their relative's grave. It took me some time to understand that the beautiful thing I could feel was the absence of fear. All were sad, but no one, young or old, seemed afraid. Grief and fear were so confused in my mind that I had accepted that they belonged together. That day, I saw that it need not be so.

When one of the mourners spoke later of his morning prayer, thanking God for granting him another day, he gave me a clue to their confidence. Unwittingly, he challenged the self-conscious intellectualizing of faith and the attempts at control in which I was embroiled as an earnest curate.

Meanwhile, growing into parenthood, I found that our children's sleepiness exemplified the surrender and pathos that embarrass me, and yet are still, I long to admit, at the core of my adult being. Thanks to electric light, bedside radios and books, we can keep at bay the thought that sleep is a powerful metaphor for death. Until the last moment before sleep, we are able to keep our sense of control, of intellectual wakefulness and confidence that we are alive and not alone. But, if that host of mourners was right, it might be enriching, not frightening, to explore the implications of night's stillness.

Like death, there is something disturbing, yet fascinating, about the way sleep enfolds us, not allowing us to analyse it as it is happening to us. Like death, sleep levels us, revealing our human vulnerability. The *Te lucis* seemed to bring together these existential themes, and I began to sing it with the children.

A number of different translations exist, of which one of the best known is by J. M. Neale (*New English Hymnal*, no. 241, and *Common Worship*, page 90); there is also a modern version on page 82 of *Common Worship*. The hymn forms part of compline (night prayer).

The words create a late-evening space for reflection. Their disarming understatement leads us from control to vulnerability, from day to night, from busy intellect to trusting heart. With nearly sentimental rhyme, they raise a childlike trust, while one of the wistful, subdued tunes to which it can be sung – Plainsong, mode 8 – carries the prayer in faith rather than certainty.

Calm, assured, yet with longing, the first verse names the twilight moment, the Creator, and then our need and his capacity to meet it. The second verse candidly describes that need. As wakeful adults, we rarely admit to having nightmares. In the space that this prayer creates for vulnerability, we find that the blurred boundary between day and night, wakefulness and sleep, is also a place where public confidence and inner doubt, belief and unbelief, can meet, embrace, and tease each other. In sleepiness, our certainties and hidden fears can converse, like acquaintances who share too much over a late-night drink.

In daytime, for example, I tend to intellectualize evil, treating it as an adjective rather than a noun. In this twilight stillness, however, the day's countless threats to our humanity and compassion are allowed to merge and be personified with all the poetic power of 'the evil foe'.

If the middle verse is too honest, too vulnerable, then the last verse firmly, but still longingly, sets our mortal selves in the reassuring context of God's eternity, with the same elusive confidence of those mourners, who would not have found peace had they not honestly faced mortality.

I admit that prayer with my children may at times be cosiness posing as piety, and the tune appeals to the comfortable part of me that loves to have a taste of monastic culture without the sacrifice. But, as night closes in, death's favourite metaphor now appears rather beautiful.

God has heard my anxiety and reminded me that such vulnerability makes me human. He has helped me to see professionalism in the context of vulnerability rather than seeing moments of openness as mere interludes in otherwise controlled or controlling conduct. God has shown me the grandeur of his eternity, in which days and nights and lives are set. I realize, now, why my Jamaican friend could say his morning thanksgiving without fear.

David Warbrick

Watch with those who wake

Watch, Lord,
with those who wake or watch or weep tonight,
and give your angels charge over those who sleep.
Tend your sick ones, O Lord Jesus Christ;
rest your weary ones;
bless your dying ones;
soothe your suffering ones;
pity your afflicted ones;
shield your joyous ones.
And all for your love's sake. Amen.

Compline collect

My grandma is a marvellous old lady, forthright of opinion and cheerful of disposition. She told me recently how she often has trouble sleeping, and how annoyed she gets to find herself wide awake in the middle of the night. Unable to nod off, she listens to the World Service.

'Do you know?' she told me. 'There are so many dreadful things happening to people in the world today in places I'd never even heard of. Nobody tells you about them in the ordinary news.' Worrying about these people doesn't help her get back to sleep, of course, but at least she hears their stories, and prays for them.

I came to know this prayer from compline at theological college (there is another version of it on page 346 of *Common Worship: Daily Prayer*). At the very end of the day, in the candle-lit chapel, the animated debates came to a quiet end in plainsong and psalm, and this prayer was offered. For me, it presented an opportunity to step beyond the world I knew, and offer a prayer for the many millions in the world for whom God has constant care and compassion.

This is a prayer for all those people who share their stories with my grandma in the silent hours of the night through the medium of the World Service. It is a prayer for all whose nights are spent in fear or hunger or illness. And it calls to mind that truism of hospitals and hospices that people are most likely to die in the earliest hours of the morning, the darkest part of the night.

It is also a prayer for the people, like my grandma, who are unable to sleep, either because their bodies won't allow them, or because there are things to worry about, racing round their minds. How often it is that, when our bodies are still, our minds amplify the nagging doubts and fears. The darkness of night and the quietness of the world force us to confront what lies within ourselves, which, at various times in our lives, is not easy.

This is also a prayer for those of us who sleep well, with full bellies and pleasant dreams. Even in our relative good fortune, we too are under God's care, shielded in our joy and watched over by the angels. We are not ignored by the divine compassion just because we are healthy and restful.

Praying this prayer, in times of contentment and plenty, gives us an opportunity to step beyond our own lives, to thank God for our joys, and to ponder for a moment those whose lives are filled with darkness, sadness and pain. We may have specific people in mind as we pray, or we may not. But we can be sure that there will be many people we do not know, for whom daytime means soldiering on and for whom the night brings a deepening of sadness.

The lives of these people may be hidden away in bald statistics in the smallest paragraphs in the middle of a newspaper, but, to God, each one is a precious child. At the end of each day, as we prepare for a good night's sleep, we hold before God those millions we do not know, and whose lives we can often only imagine, hoping as we pray that they may be aware that they, and we, are never abandoned by the God who walks close by – watching, tending, resting, blessing, soothing and loving.

Georgina Byrne

Bear each other's burdens

My God, I pray not for myself alone,
but for him who is as dear to me as my own soul.
Suffer us, till life ceases, to bear each other's burdens.
Knit our hearts together in steadfast love.
May we walk together in the narrow way,
upheld by mutual prayer, and our children with us.
Perfect in heaven the love begun on earth.
Smite us in an eternal bond,
and let nothing put asunder those whom thou hast joined together.

Josephine Butler (1828–1906)

Josephine Butler's prayer, written for her husband George, seems like a pleasantly measured petition for commitment and mutual support in their life together. It is biblical in its echoes of the narrow way of Matthew 7, the mutual prayer of Ecclesiastes 4, and the shared burdens of Galatians 6. It echoes the marriage service of the Book of Common Prayer.

Although it is generally applicable to any couple contemplating or already engaged in marriage, there appears nothing particularly special about it: it is neither as eloquent as many of the collects of the Prayer Book, nor, on the surface, personal enough to offer a window on to the life of a great Victorian Christian social reformer.

Yet behind the generality is a particular tragedy, and in the plea for continued faithfulness is a knowledge of desperate sadness, which make this prayer moving and profound. Josephine and George's six-year-old daughter Eva died in 1863, after she fell down the stairs.

Josephine's biographer Jane Jordan records how, not long after Eva's death, Josephine found George alone and pale, and forced him to talk cheerfully of their daughter. The prayer refers to him in this place of grief, and hints at Josephine's fear that she might lose her husband as well as her daughter.

This is not a prayer about the loss of a child, though; it is a prayer for a deeply loved husband, about marriage that is coloured by loss. It does not seek to minimize the pain of his grief, but it reminds him of the solid foundations on which their life together, and with their remaining children, is built.

It offers hope that they will be reunited with Eva, but balances the consolation of heaven with the steadfast commitments of life now. And, without naming George's imprisonment in grief, it models how love can take you out of yourself when you care more for the other than for yourself: 'I pray not for myself alone,' she begins, setting aside her own temptation to introspection or even self-pity at this point.

When we love God and love another, we can long for that person's happiness, and share his or her sorrow in a way that makes us more fully human. Josephine Butler herself suggested that her later work with prostitutes and the destitute was fired by her loss: she wrote that she 'became possessed with an irresistible urge to go forth and find some pain keener than my own, to meet with people more unhappy than myself'.

Here, though, when her grief is still raw, she turns first to the love of her husband, which has sustained her in her public and private life, and to living with the grief that only they, as Eva's parents, fully share. She offers him a prayer, which, we must imagine, she has already prayed for him, perhaps in the hope that he will pray it for her, and that God will help them both lead each other on from sorrow to new life.

This is a model of marriage: each carries the other, each is sustained by the other, and God is at the centre. Whether we are contemplating the shared history of our own relationship in marriage, or seeing others undertake that commitment afresh, we can be reminded by this prayer's generous commitment – particularly if we have our own experience of loss – that in bearing one another's burdens we are trying to do for each other what God already does for us.

Joanne Woolway Grenfell

Pilgrimage and perseverance

May the road rise to meet you

May the road rise to meet you,
May the wind be always at your back,
May the sun shine warm upon your face,
May the rains fall softly upon your fields.
Until we meet again,
May God hold you in the hollow of his hand.

Traditional Celtic

This Celtic blessing, of unknown origin, has become a favourite in recent years. It is wonderfully evocative. Unlike many prayers, the words build a picture. They conjure up a place in one's imagination: a place that feeds the senses, where one can see and hear, touch, and even smell the presence of God.

I wonder whether we always use the range of our senses as we might when we pray. This prayer encourages us to feel God – to feel his touch in the breeze of the wind, the warmth of the sun, and the gentleness of the rain; and, perhaps more importantly, to feel his protective hold. The last line is reminiscent of those verses from Psalm 139 that describe the intimacy with which God knows us, and the hand of God that holds us. It suggests how uniquely precious each and every one of us is to God.

When our first child, Hannah, was stillborn, a friend sent me a photo of a sculpture by a German artist, Dorothea Steigerwald, of a child being cradled in the palm of God's hand. As I was unable to protect our daughter myself, this image has remained with me ever since, and provided much comfort. Probably because of this association, I now frequently use this blessing at funerals, because I believe it speaks to a need.

When someone close to us dies, it can be the loss of touch that hurts us most – being unable to feel her skin or the warmth of her breath. This blessing, so rich in its imagery, addresses that pain – often unarticulated – because it attaches importance to the physical. Implicit in its expression is an understanding of our need for physical comfort, and our desire that those we love, living and departed, should be party to that comfort, too.

The interrelationship between the physical and spiritual world in Celtic spirituality leaves no place for the dichotomy between spirit and matter that exists in other strands of Christian thinking. Instead, nature in all its glorious passion is appreciated as God's gift. Nature communicates with us, and draws us closer to our maker. In the elements, we meet our creator.

In the opening line, it is the earth – the road – that rises to meet us. For me, these words suggest a further image, that of the forgiving father, who spots his prodigal son from far away, and goes to meet him; or the beautifully crafted lines of the post-communion prayer: 'when we were still far off you met us in your Son and brought us home'.

These lines also convey an understanding of life as a journey, where God meets us along the way. Each line points beyond itself – the wind to God's spirit; the warmth of the sun to God's light; and the softness of the rain to God's compassion, for God deals gently with the dreams we nurture (our fields).

However we choose to use this prayer, perhaps its greatest value – and its challenge to us – lies in its appreciation of this world as an expression of the divine.

Annabel Shilson-Thomas

May He support us

May He support us all the day long,
till the shades lengthen
and the evening comes,
and the busy world is hushed,
and the fever of life is over
and our work is done!
Then in His Mercy
may He give us a safe lodging
and a holy rest
and peace at the last.

John Henry Newman (1801–90)

When I was training for ordination, I lived in a house in Beswick, Manchester, with four other ordinands, each on a different placement in the city. At the end of the working day, we would gather for the evening Office, bringing our thoughts about the people we had met and our varied experiences.

During that time, I learned from another student, who had been a nun, something of how to pray as a religious community for the community outside. She prayed for those who were travelling home from work; for those who were setting off to work the night shift; for those for whom that night would be their last. She prayed for those who were lonely, and those who would die alone.

When I read Newman's prayer, I am taken back to that sense of a city going to sleep, the blood draining from its heart as people make their way from its centre to its suburbs. I feel again the sound of trams and the wail of police cars still singing in my ears, and the connection between our individual day ending and the collective bustle of a city day slowing, dispersing, and settling into the quieter heartbeat of those who keep the night watch.

The more obvious setting for the prayer is the shadows lengthening and the evening drawing in around the heady scent of honeysuckle in Oriel College's second quad during Newman's university teaching days in Oxford. But the point is that this is a prayer for the ending of any day, anywhere, and with it the ending of any life. It is a prayer that asks for a good and peaceful end. It asks us to remember that we should be attentive each day to the possibility that this day is our last.

It isn't a prayer that asks us to live in fear of dying or of judgement, but it does encourage us to find some sense of resolution at the end of each day, as a preparation for the resolution we might hope to feel when our life's work is over. So our completed day becomes a microcosm of our completed life, and helps us to long for rest and eternal dwelling with God, as naturally as we long for the comfort of our beds after the busyness and the conversations of each day have come to an end.

The rhythm of the prayer guides our bodily responses into a physical calmness, in the knowledge that our spirit will often follow our body. The four 'and's which begin the third to sixth lines make us slow our breathing so that we become aware of a change of pace. By the sixth line, we are slowed further, and brought almost to a standstill by the last word, 'done'. It is as if someone has taken out of our hands that one last thing that we want to do before we stop our work, and has told us that we really have done enough.

The seventh line takes us on to a different plane, with its calm and resolved opening 'then', leading us into God's merciful presence, and ushering us into the petition of the final lines. Perhaps only by then are we beginning to realize we need to offer these words – for lodging, rest and peace. I always want to read this prayer twice, the second time with the calmness of mind that the first time's reading has brought about.

My husband's granny has this prayer by her bed. Old age might sharpen our focus about needing to still our souls in readiness for God, but youth can appreciate the habit of seeking resolution of, and respite from, all that keeps us busy.

Joanne Woolway Grenfell

Through perils unknown

Lord God,
you have called your servants
to ventures of which we cannot see the ending,
by paths as yet untrodden,
through perils unknown.
Give us faith to go out with good courage,
not knowing where we go,
but only that your hand is leading us
and your love supporting us;
through Jesus Christ our Lord.
Amen.

From *The Lutheran Book of Worship*

This prayer has guided me through the odd peril. It was said regularly by a Lutheran student with whom I said morning prayer for several years. Her fragile circumstances but steely commitment represented a vivid illustration of the theme. No doubt she repeated it to sustain her own faith and courage – little realizing what inspiration it offered to those around her.

I think of this prayer particularly at New Year, when new resolutions abound. The prayer takes me back to some golden old ones, the very basics for living and loving, as I look ahead to a year that I must greet as a stranger. I've stepped out in faith before, and I've trusted the God who leads and loves before, but I need to be reminded to do so again; and again. Life is complicated, and I value this prayer to bring me back to the simple truths, at least annually, and preferably daily.

'You have called your servants to ventures': I'm reminded first that God's call involves a journey. So each year will not be the same as the past one, and I must look to God afresh. We are 'pilgrims', called to 'progress'. At times, the demands may feel excessive and the risks foolish, but God's choice for us involves the excitement of adventure over the comfort of safety, any day.

'By paths as yet untrodden': I'm reminded, second, that I am called to walk with God on my own path. Or, rather, on the path he gives to me. Others may offer advice from the perspective of their path – and there may be companions treading parallel paths – but my path will be different. I am uniquely created and named by God. 'He made you like this because he wanted one like you,' as a friend puts it. So I am uniquely called and equipped: how silly of me, then, to attempt walking along someone else's way.

Such a calling is daunting – me, a pioneer? – but the third prompt, an acknowledgement of ignorance, helps (strangely) to quell my queasiness. 'We cannot see the ending . . . perils unknown.' Christopher Columbus is reputed to have written again and again in his journal: 'No land in sight. Kept sailing.' Our destination, in worldly terms, is unclear. The calling is to keep going: to keep setting out in faith. Here is relief.

I suspect my Lutheran student friend would never have set out on her studies if she had known what pitfalls lay ahead; but, with hindsight, she is glad she did. Especially when the perils outnumber the joys, one day at a time is quite enough. Ignorance is bliss, when it comes to whether the doctoral research is eventually fruitful, or the medication effective, or the distant job possibility real.

Beyond such ephemeral concerns, of course, Christians are those who do know where they are going. Christians are those who see the wider canvas; those entrusted with the news of how God's salvation story ends; those who look to the final act of the play, in which God sweeps up all the loose strands out of which the new heaven and new earth is revealed. Against this backdrop, our individual journeys seem very minor – simply the weaving of individual strands – and their end points seem almost irrelevant.

The final reminder involves an underlining of the certainties to which we can cling while en route: God's guiding hand and his supporting love. These are not the far-distant 'encouragements' of a deist God: they are the concrete realities of a God whose hands bear the scars of nails, whose love was demonstrated through infinitely greater peril than we can ever know. Through Jesus Christ our Lord. Amen.

Jo Bailey Wells

Pilgrim God

Pilgrim God, bless us with courage, where our way is fraught with
  danger
Bless us with good companions, where the way demands a common
  cause
Bless us with good humour, for we cannot travel lightly
  when weighed down with over-much solemnity
Bless us with humility to learn from those around us
Bless us with decisiveness, when we have to move quickly
Bless our lazy moments, when we need to stretch our limbs for the
  journey
Bless us, lead us, love us and bring us home, bearing the gospel of life.

Anonymous

This prayer will always for me be associated with my five years as a
member of the chapter of Canterbury Cathedral. It was used at a deanery
pilgrimage, and seemed to combine the perennial image of pilgrimage
with the contemporary need for lightness of touch in our religious ob-
servances.

I always felt it was a great privilege to say morning prayer five yards
from the spot where Thomas Becket was murdered on that grim December afternoon in 1170. From that day on, millions of people have made
their pilgrimage to Canterbury – from Henry II, barefoot and penitent,
to coachloads of French schoolchildren with Nike trainers and fistfuls of
euros.

There were many like a man I came across in the cloisters who said to
me with great simplicity: 'A few years ago this place saved my life. I was
at the end of the road, and it saved me.'

Pilgrimage may seem like an overworked metaphor for the Christian
life, but this prayer gives it some fresh clothing. Good companions and
good humour go together, but, whatever Chaucer's Canterbury pilgrims
got up to, good humour isn't always what the secular world associates
with the Church. Spike Milligan longed for just one passage in the Bible
along the lines of: 'Jesus sayeth – come unto me and I will tell you a joke.'
But no such luck, he concluded sadly. Humour is a humanizing gift; it's
worth praying for.

I also like the balance between decisiveness and laziness – both important for the journey. The art is to know which is appropriate when;

but, in an increasingly frenetic culture, both are necessary. The need to fill every unforgiving hour with purposeful activity looks increasingly pathological, but it is the chosen course of so many of us. 'Bless our lazy moments,' and enable us to recreate our inner harmonies. Ultimately, we ask to be brought home to God, in that faith-filled phrase, 'bearing the gospel of life'.

This prayer, above all, affirms life. It bounces between realism ('fraught with danger', 'over-much solemnity') and lightness of touch ('travel lightly', 'stretch our limbs'). It constantly asks for blessing, but only so that we might be more fully alive to God's gifts for us.

'It has long been my conviction', said Bishop John V. Taylor, 'that God is not hugely concerned as to whether we are religious or not. What matters to God, and matters supremely, is whether we are alive or not.' May our pilgrimage daily bring us to life – for the sake of the world.

John Pritchard

Seeking your face

Eternal Light, shine in our hearts;
Eternal Goodness, deliver us from evil;
Eternal Power, be our support;
Eternal Wisdom, scatter the darkness of our ignorance;
Eternal Pity, have mercy upon us:
that with all our heart and mind
and soul and strength
we may seek your face
and be brought by your infinite mercy
to your holy presence:
through Jesus Christ our Lord.

Alcuin of York (c.735–804)

Alcuin was born in or near the city of York, the son of an ancient Northumbrian family. He entered the cathedral school as a child, and finally became the master there. In 781 he went to Aachen as master of the palace school, and adviser on religion and education in the court of Charlemagne.

Although he was not a monk and only a deacon, he was made Abbot of Tours in 796, and he remained there for the eight years until he died. Alcuin wrote poetry and prayers, compiled a sacramentary, revised the lectionary, and was involved in liturgical reform.

In 793 Alcuin wrote from Aachen to Higbald, the Bishop of Lindisfarne, offering his sympathy on the sack of Lindisfarne by the Danes on 8 June that year. In this letter, he describes Lindisfarne as the 'holiest place in Britain'. He also exhorts the survivors: 'Let us love what is eternal, and not what is perishable. Let us esteem true riches, not fleeting ones; eternal, not transitory ones.'

I often use this prayer of Alcuin's because of its positive attitude to the eternal presence. I think that the modern idea of positive thinking is positively stupid. Prayers, Alcuin's included, are not just positive thinking; they are tuning in to the reality that God is with us. God comes to us, and desires that we turn to him.

As the prayer begins with Eternal Light and asks Eternal Wisdom to 'scatter the darkness', I often use this as a candle-lighting prayer. I prefer to start in total darkness, which is the situation of our life without God, and then ask for God's eternal light to shine upon us.

During the season of Easter, as I light the candle I also use the words: 'Jesus Christ is the Light of the world. Alleluia,' with the response: 'A light that no darkness can put out.' I end the candle-lighting with the words: 'May the Christ risen in glory scatter the darkness from our hearts and minds and from this world. Alleluia, Amen.'

To our darkness comes the light of God; to our sinfulness comes God's goodness and forgiveness; to our weakness comes his power and support; to our foolishness and lack of awareness comes the eternal wisdom of God. At all times, God's great mercy is offered to us. God asks that we seek him with our whole being, until we come at the last to the fullness of his glory. These are wonderful truths, but we need to take time each day to make them ours.

As life is a pilgrimage and a journeying deeper into our awareness of the ever-abiding presence, I have given this prayer to many pilgrims and seekers. It is a good prayer for daily use: it expresses well our searching for God, and God's eternal coming to us.

David Adam

The Lord bless you

May the Lord bless your ears,
  that you may hear his Word.
May the Lord bless your eyes,
  that you may see his light.
May the Lord bless your lips,
  that you may respond to his love.
May the Lord bless your heart,
  that he may dwell there for ever.
May the Lord bless your shoulders,
  that you may carry his cross
  and live always by its saving power.
Amen.

Anonymous

Saying goodbye to someone we love for the last time is never easy. Most of us long to keep our friendships, and find that the day someone moves is a day of real loss.

At its most extreme, I remember an account of how parents would run alongside the trains of those emigrating from the west of Ireland at the end of the nineteenth century. It saddens me every time I read it:

> A deafening wail resounds as the station bell gives the signal of starting. I have seen grey-haired peasants so clutch and cling to a departing child at this last moment that only the utmost force of three or four friends could tear them apart.
>
> When at last the train moves away, amidst a scene of passionate grief, hundreds run along the fields beside the line to catch a glimpse of the friends they shall see no more. (L. M. Cullen, *Life in Ireland*, Batsford, 1968)

In our city parishes today, the moving away of familiar members of the congregation can seem distressing. Some cities are experiencing a new wave of economic migration, as wealthier families move away from urban centres, attracted by the quality and benefits of smaller-town life. How do others, who cannot and do not wish to move, respond?

We are aware of the economic pressures on those of us who remain, and it would be easy to resent the decisions made by such émigrés. Or we could draw from another Irish tradition. If you stand among the ruins of the great monastery at Clonmacnoise, close to the brooding waters of the river Shannon, you might wish to recall how this thriving community, 1,000 years ago, had at its core a huge guesthouse.

Hospitality was a key feature of such places. Bede writes that scholars and beggars, orphans and adulterers were all welcomed to share 'the clean house with its big fire, washing and bathing and a couch without sorrow'. Within the tradition, there was the assumption that while people would come, they would also go, and the community was to be as positive about the sending out as it had been warm in its welcome.

I discovered this anonymous blessing on a service sheet in Salford Roman Catholic Cathedral. It has become a favourite text in our parish at the first public service at which our confirmation candidates are presented to the congregation for their prayer support. It is spoken slowly and deliberately, as each candidate is given a pocket-sized cross to carry on his or her journey.

We do not know when the prayer was written, but, with a little imagination, one can hear the same words being spoken to those who stood on the banks of the Shannon, who might have had rather more reason to be fearful than the average confirmation candidate.

It can give us encouragement when we think of Ascension and Pentecost. In a strange way, Jesus' disciples were beginning to find his occasional appearances, after his resurrection, somewhat reassuring and almost normal. Yet Jesus had come to the conclusion that they were now ready to let him go.

The future of the Church, especially in our cities, continues to be fragile, and new ways will have to emerge. This is not the time to hold on to former members in the hope that the present can continue: now is the time for Christ to bless our shoulders, 'that we may carry his cross and live always by its saving power'.

John Burniston

I bind unto myself

I bind unto myself today
The strong name of the Trinity,
By invocation of the same,
The Three in One and One in Three.
I bind this day to me for ever,
By power of faith, Christ's incarnation;
His baptism in Jordan river;
His death on Cross for my salvation;
His bursting from the spiced tomb;
His riding up the heavenly way;
His coming at the day of doom;
I bind unto myself today.

St Patrick's Breastplate
(ascribed to St Patrick, 372–466,
translated by Mrs C. F. Alexander)

St Patrick's Breastplate (or, rather, Cecil Frances Alexander's fluent development of it) caught me just when it was needed, on the night before my ordination as a priest 50 years ago. It has been my first morning prayer ever since. We sang it (though, sadly, not all nine verses) when I was consecrated bishop.

Fifty years ago I had never heard of Celtic spirituality. The *Breastplate* affirms the central truths of God as Trinity and of Christ's incarnation. It affirms God's presence in this world of creation. If this is Celtic, so be it. To me, it's normal orthodoxy. But then, as a Welshman, I would say that, wouldn't I?

I bind to myself. I claim as my protection, as my identity. With this defence, I can defy the assumptions and priorities that will come at me during the day, from outside myself and from within. I was most consciously claiming this defence when I was in a community of Christians who were trying to work out their commitment and obedience amid the heresies and cruelties of South Africa during the years of apartheid. But the basic claims remain valid, wherever we are.

I claim the truth of God as Trinity. In a world in which power is exercised from above downwards, with few at the top and many at the bottom, I claim the nature of God as community. At the heart of all things, the motive of power is subservient to the motive of love; the motive of competition is less real than the motive of co-operation; the motive of purity-by-exclusion is secondary to the motive of holiness-by-inclusion.

During the day, I may at times feel afraid of losing my support from other people. I may hesitate to take on a commitment that might require me to stand alone. I may want to avoid the risk of isolation. My binding to the Trinity gives me confidence that I will not be fundamentally isolated. The bondedness of the One-in-Three is a guarantee that bondedness is at the heart of the universe. So I can take the risk.

Or, on another day, I may feel threatened by the sense that I am just part of a general human mass, without any distinctiveness or personal quality. I may be tempted to parade myself with some special achievement or eccentricity or minority identity. My binding to God as Trinity gives me confidence that I am still unique, and I do not need to resort to such tricks. The diversity within the Three-in-One is a guarantee that distinctiveness is at the heart of the universe. I do not have to prove myself more clever or holy or racially pure than anyone else.

In the heart of God, separateness ('apartheid' in Afrikaans) is overcome, and distinctiveness is vindicated.

I bind to myself today Christ's incarnation. Against much of the immediate evidence, I recognize that God has claimed this world as a fitting place for God to be in. The conventions of society and religion may make me feel that God, if there is a God, has to be way beyond the highest levels of human status, and that any organization representing God will have to be a device for congratulating the powerful on being powerful. But a day when I bind Christ's incarnation to myself will be a day when I will watch for Christ at the bottom of the human pyramid. I will watch for the signs of a God whose hands have been damaged by nails, as anyone's hands would be damaged.

In the power of God as Trinity, in the power of Christ incarnate, I have a daily commitment to holy defiance.

John D. Davies

Know thee more dearly

Thanks be to thee, my Lord Jesus Christ:
for all the benefits which thou hast given me;
for all the pains and insults which thou hast borne for me.
O most merciful Redeemer, friend and brother:
may I know thee more clearly,
love thee more dearly,
and follow thee more nearly,
for ever and ever. Amen.

St Richard of Chichester (1197–1253) and
Eric Milner-White (1884–1963)

The life of St Richard records him as having uttered the first sentence of
this prayer on his deathbed. What is touching about the first sentence is
the sense of gratitude it exhibits. Here is a powerful man coming to the
end of his life, a man who had been Chancellor of Oxford University and
Canterbury, then the bishop of a large and important see, who at the end
is only concerned to give thanks for the benefits that Christ had brought
him. It is known that Richard was a man of deep spirituality: these final
words show that, however far he had come, what truly mattered was
Christ's redeeming love for him, and he is thankful.

The second sentence of the prayer and the ending seem to have been
added in the early twentieth century. These lines, which we know so well,
are first found in a book of prayers compiled by G. R. Bullock-Webster in
1915. The last line was added by Eric Milner-White. Even if they are not
by Richard himself, they echo his thinking about Christ the Redeemer.
Though he didn't say these words, he could well have done.

I remember this prayer as one of the first that I ever memorized as a
young Christian – probably like many others. Chichester was not far
from my home on the Isle of Wight, and my parents often took me there,
so the prayer was naturally part of my early faith. But, looking back on it
now, I am struck by the way in which Christ is called 'friend and brother'
well before such a personal way of talking about Christ became more
familiar and accepted. St John clearly sanctions the word friend (John
15.14–15), but it is not so well remembered that St Paul calls Christ 'the

first of many brothers' in Romans (8.29), where it is often translated 'first of a big family'.

It is important that this prayer, with its deep sense of the proximity of Christ's redemption and the personal and intimate nature of that redemption, remains in our consciousness. There is a great deal of talk in the contemporary Church about Christ as 'Lord' and 'King'. This risks portraying Christ in an overbearing, patriarchal way. It can work against the evangelism it seeks to further.

If we spoke more clearly of Christ as 'merciful Redeemer, friend and brother', then we would not only be following in the footsteps of Richard of Chichester and Aelred of Rievaulx, but we might also be able to speak of him more effectively to so many people who are longing for intimacy and friendship in their lives.

Melvyn Matthews

For all the saints

For all the saints
    who went before us,
    who have spoken to our hearts
    and touched us with your fire,
    we praise you, O God.

For all the saints
    who live beside us
    whose weaknesses and strengths
    are woven with our own,
    we praise you, O God.

For all the saints
    who live beyond us
    who challenge us
    to change the world with them,
    we praise you, O God.

Janet Morley, from *Bread of Tomorrow*

The prayers that Janet Morley has written manage to combine seeming simplicity with spiritual depth. They are beautifully crafted and work well in public worship and private prayer. In this prayer, we give thanks for being a people in community. As Christians, we are connected to those who have gone before, those who are near at hand, and those who are living out their faith in ways that are different and at times challenging. It reminds me of Dag Hammarskjöld's lines: 'For all that has been – Thanks! For all that shall be – Yes!'

The term 'saints' here echoes the New Testament use of fellow Christians rather than those who have been formally canonized, though it can encompass them, too. We begin with those who have gone before.

It is always good to remember our inheritance of faith, the individuals and communities who inspired our own journey. It is also important to know the stories of faithful people from the past, to tell the tales of men and women who lived for the gospel. We live out our Christian faith, building on the foundations others have laid, rejoicing in freedoms others have won, inspired by the visions that others have worked for. For all that has been – Thanks.

The prayer then reminds us that we live among saints, and that saints are not perfect. These are the people whose 'weaknesses and strengths are woven with our own'. We are called to live out our Christian faith in community, and we need to rejoice in the people who walk beside us; to rejoice in the people who support us in our weaknesses, and whom we support with our strengths.

As we look around the particular Christian communities in which we worship and work, it is important that we acknowledge that we share the sanctifying gift of the Holy Spirit. We are not expected to do it alone, but always in our praying and discipleship to be supported by our fellow saints.

The prayer ends with a reminder that not all the saints are comfortable. There are those who carry out their Christian discipleship in ways that can challenge our choices and lifestyles. These are the saints who may make us question whether we are generous enough with our time, money and talents. They may help us to look again at our assumptions of what being a Christian is, and perhaps inspire us to be more open to God and to the needs of his world. Or we might simply give thanks that they have the courage to live out their faith in situations that we know we would find too hard.

This prayer is naturally used at All Saints', but it is also appropriate for any occasion when a Church is thinking about its mission. It helps us give thanks for the past, value the present, and be open to the possibility that God may challenge us to do more.

Emma Percy

May they all be one

Lord Jesus Christ, You said
May they all be one, just as, Father,
You are in me and I am in You,
So that the world might believe
It was You who sent me.

Dear Lord, bring together in love and peace
all who believe in You.
Amen.

Cardinal Basil Hume OSB (1923–99)

For six years I attended a Roman Catholic school. Despite being an Anglican, I served at the altar, and many of my friends were Roman Catholics, in varying degrees of faithfulness to the Church. Not being allowed to receive communion at mass was something that hurt: it made me stand out and feel frustrated. But it also had a far more important effect: it made me realize that the disunity of Christians is scandalous.

Cardinal Hume's prayer helps us to understand why this is so. Unity is not simply about being nice to one another, or coming together for administrative or pragmatic reasons. In his so-called high priestly prayer in John's Gospel, Jesus prays for the unity of his followers in order that the world might believe (John 17). This is the prime reason for the unity of Christians, which Cardinal Hume highlights in this prayer: that the world may come to faith in Jesus Christ. Put bluntly, the core vocation of the Church is to make Jesus Christ known, and to lead the world to fullness of life in him.

In order to do this, we need to consider carefully what unity is really about. Cardinal Hume's successor at Westminster, Cardinal Cormac Murphy-O'Connor, has said: 'Ecumenism is like a road with no exit. There is no going back.'

But there is also no quick fix. Our ecumenical discussions are too often characterized by nervousness about difference, and a desire to see everyone as the same, thus somehow solving the problem. But this reflects neither the messy reality of Christians' lives nor the glory of the ecumenical vocation to which the Church is called irreversibly.

In Jesus' high priestly Prayer, which Cardinal Hume quotes, the kind of unity Jesus beseeches for his followers is a radical one. 'May they be one, Father, just as You are in me and I am in You.' This is not a unity of the lowest common denominator, nor simply of friendship. Rather, it has a futuristic quality about it that can be fully realized only at the end of time: that together we might be fully united in and with Christ.

A straw poll will show you that it is impossible to get the smallest number of people to agree fully about anything – let alone all Christians (or even all Anglicans). But there is a deeper unity than this, which may be able to contain such difference, and which is contained in our baptism.

As we already share this intimate bond of unity, let's try to lose some of our institutionalized nervousness and the temptation to turn 'the other' into a carbon copy of ourselves. This is merely to deny the diversity of God's creation, and turn our vision of unity into an idol. Cardinal Hume's prayer teaches us that the initiative for unity is God's. Despite all our striving for unity, it is God's gift, and will be accomplished through his grace.

But this is not a call to complacency – far from it. Our inaction as well as our action can frustrate God's will. Rather, it's about learning to see the other as he or she really is, and then having the courage to be honest about our differences. If we are to have open hearts and minds to see where the Spirit might lead the Church to unity, it will involve real listening, attentive prayer and wise discernment.

All of this, costly though it will be, is for one reason: so that we can offer a more coherent and dynamic picture to the world of lives transformed by the Spirit of the Risen Christ, 'that the world might believe'.

Jamie Hawkey

Prayer

Prayer the Churches banquet, Angels age,
   Gods breath in man returning to his birth,
   The soul in paraphrase, heart in pilgrimage,
The Christian plummet sounding heav'n and earth;
Engine against th' Almightie, sinners towre,
   Reversed thunder, Christ-side-piercing spear,
   The six-daies world transposing in an houre,
A kind of tune, which all things heare and fear;
Softnesse, and peace, and joy, and love, and blisse,
   Exalted Manna, gladnesse of the best,
   Heaven in ordinarie, man well drest,
The milkie way, the bird of Paradise,
   Church-bels beyond the starres heard, the souls bloud,
   The land of spices; something understood.

George Herbert (1593–1633)

When I feel that my words aren't adequate to address God, this poem gives my feelings wings and sends a shiver down my spine. It's a poem about the language of prayer, but which, at its heart, is about how God is revealed in the ordinariness of everyday experience, in a way that makes all things special.

So this isn't an exercise in finding words that sound right, but is a yearning to express all that we feel about the Almighty – a quest for meaning, a journey into our desire to express how we experience God around us. It shows us that when we really search, 'heart in pilgrimage', the process of searching is sometimes where we find the answer. And it's a poem that, in its grasping after lived truth, becomes a prayer in its own right.

In looking at 'Prayer' as a poem, many critics have noted its central theme of finding 'Heaven in ordinarie', and have shown how George Herbert's poetry is adept at using everyday language to describe spiritual experience. But, as a prayer that we might use ourselves, it is perhaps most successful not in creating a language with which to pray, but in heightening the senses to help us see how observing what is around us can bring us closer to God.

I remember attending an Easter vigil when I initially felt I was so caught up in the ordinary that I was quite immune to the spiritual. Then I recall entering a state of extraordinary sensory acuity, which reminded me that ordinary and spiritual are not opposites. There was the sizzling of water extinguishing the baptism candle; the insistent drone of sirens up the busy arterial road outside; someone's perfume; a friend's obviously new shoes – all made me glad to be part of this worshipping community, and seemed to offer signposts to God.

I sense that Herbert was in a similarly heightened state when he wrote this prayer. All the senses are switched on: sight, hearing, and smell most obviously, but even touch in the 'Christ-side-piercing spear', and taste in the 'exalted Manna'. Time and space, history, astronomy and geography are onlookers, and the human form – its heart, soul, blood and breath – embodies our connection with God, and helps us reach out to make that connection from the physical world we inhabit.

There are two other reasons why this isn't just a poem about finding the right spiritual language, but is essentially an enactment of the bodily process of praying. First, the poem hints (however much we might disagree) that the author's own expression is still only partial, presented in snatches of song and paraphrases of real meaning. Second, the poem's opening idea is that all that follows is actually God's language, divine breath breathed into a human shell, and now returned in praise to the Author.

How we come to life, and how our words come to life, seem to be connected, and it is in Herbert's attempt to articulate this process that this poem becomes a prayer. As prayer is the Church's banquet, so this feast of words is a thanksgiving for our world and our ability to observe and comprehend, a hymn of gratitude for the 'land of spices; something understood'.

Joanne Woolway Grenfell

Nada de turba

Let nothing disturb you,
nothing affright you;
all things are passing,
God never changes.
Patient endurance
attains unto all things;
who God possesses
in nothing is wanting:
alone God suffices.

St Teresa of Avila (1515–82)

In my mind, this is the prayer of three holy women, one of whom I knew when I was a small boy, and another when I was a student. It was written by the third: Teresa of Avila, a Carmelite nun of the sixteenth century, about whom great books have deservedly been written.

My mother started going to church (and encouraged me to go) when I was about seven years old. The Vicar was on the high side, but there was an elderly server who was very high indeed. His wife was severely incapacitated by arthritis, and we used to visit her.

What do I remember about this old lady? 'Patient endurance attains unto all things.' She embodied patience. She had to have so many things done for her: shopping, cooking, cleaning, personal hygiene. Surrender of areas that have been your domain is not easy.

Then there was the time factor. She had too much of it: hours alone and little means of justifying one's existence by productivity. But I learned that she did something to 'redeem' the time: she prayed. I think that's why we and others visited. She gave us quality experience of unde-monstrative prayer in pain and love, making the tiny sitting room of her council bungalow a gate of heaven.

If you face illness, old age, or incapacity that demands the surrender of your control over life, you can surrender, too, a torrent of prayer to God, and throw into it all the energies of your lost endeavours.

The second holy woman is a nun. A group of us met her when we were training for the priesthood. She, like Teresa of Avila, was a Carmelite, but an Anglican one. She spoke to us about prayer in the depths of the night, a hidden activity in which her community offered to God the darkness hours that unleashed crime, heart-rending degradation – of oneself and others – and death. She powerfully described her 'enclosure' in terms that presented it as an oblation of prayer that engaged with the demons: 'principalities and powers', in Pauline terms.

Years later I met her again on a return visit to the Convent of the Incarnation at Fairacres, in Oxford. Her body was ravaged by illness, and she was slumped in a wheelchair. But, like the elderly server's wife, she had an iconic quality that made you want to fall to your knees. Her holiness was evident in the radiance of her face. She had seen heaven. God had set his seal on her, and on it was engraved: 'Let nothing disturb you.'

When your demons prowl and threaten, stand fast against them, remembering those who pray for you at night. Let nothing disturb you.

Finally, there is Teresa herself. This formidably human and impressive woman defies many stereotypes. The courage to be herself can be detected in the last line of this prayer, her 'bookmark': 'alone God suffices.'

Take time to ponder such an unqualified statement. And be glad.

Martin Warner

The Elixir

Teach me, my God and King,
In all things thee to see,
And what I do in any thing,
To do it as for thee.

George Herbert (1593–1633)

The first stanza of George Herbert's poem 'The Elixir' is better known to most of us as the first verse of a hymn. It's easy to take hymns for granted – they are, after all, often treated as the musical interludes in services. Congregations get to stand up, stretch their legs, and rifle through pockets and handbags for money, a handkerchief or a sweet – we've all done it. But hymns are most often addressed to God: they are musical prayers, and as such may be taken and made our own.

The writer of this hymn had a prestigious academic career at Cambridge in the early seventeenth century. He was ordained and in 1630 made Rector of Bemerton, a country parish just outside Salisbury, where he died of consumption in 1633. But Herbert is best remembered for his poems, which have an engaging honesty and hint at depths beneath an apparent simplicity. Others are popular as hymns, too.

This hymn begins with a plea from the singer to God. It exemplifies Herbert's extraordinary knack of putting into words an experience common to us all. As we sing and pray, we ask that in all things we might glimpse the glory of God.

The opening line is to the point: 'Teach me'. We are straightaway on familiar prayer territory: the phrase captures something of the exasperation of prayer, that real desire to see and know God more deeply, combined with the knowledge that we are usually too preoccupied, too obtuse or too dull to notice where and when God is present. We need to be taught; to be pointed in the right direction and shown. It is a humbling prayer, the prayer of one who seeks to know and love God, and to worship God, but who is acutely aware of his own inadequacy.

I meet many people who believe that, as a vicar, I've got prayer sorted. True, I say the Office with my colleagues; I offer intercessions for the sick and suffering; I spend some time in quiet contemplation, and mutter short, sharp 'arrow' prayers during times of crisis or international foot-ball matches. But do I, as St Paul commended, 'pray without ceasing'? Do I see God in all things? The honest answer is, of course, no. Like everyone else, and like George Herbert, a country parson centuries before me, I am often preoccupied or ill-disciplined.

There is no magic formula to make prayer exciting and uplifting every time. All of us have lapses in the discipline of prayer. We all fidget and find our minds wandering. Honest prayer is about returning to God, time and time again, and finding God waiting patiently for us. And, when we return for the umpteenth time to God, there is no better prayer than the opening verse of Herbert's hymn: 'Teach me'. Let me start again; start afresh.

It is a prayer that reminds us to keep persisting. To pray again, 'Teach me' is to step in the right direction when we have wandered away. As such, it is a prayer most of us need to return to at the beginning, middle and end of a life of faith. Whether or not we sing beautifully and tune-fully, this hymn is one prayer that all of us, in our heart of hearts, can take as our own.

Georgina Byrne

Continuing unto the end

O Lord God,
when thou givest to thy servants
to endeavour any great matter,
Grant us also to know that it is not the beginning,
but the continuing of the same unto the end,
until it be thoroughly finished,
which yieldeth the true glory:
through him that for the finishing of thy work laid down his life,
our Saviour Jesus Christ. Amen.

Attributed to Sir Francis Drake (c.1545–96)

It is said that this prayer was first spoken by Sir Francis Drake in 1587, as he was about to attack the Spanish fleet in Cadiz harbour. That may not appeal greatly to an era with little taste and less admiration for military or naval exploits. How can the words of a licensed killer speak to us of the purposes of God?

Whatever the details of the attribution, there is no doubt the words themselves strike a chord across a wide spectrum. Soldiers and politicians have taken it up, as have campaigners to relieve debt in developing countries. It is a natural choice before any difficult undertaking. Though our modern interpretation of 'great matter' is unlikely to include naval warfare, it could be stretched to embrace a parish project, a mission, or the launch of a development fund.

What makes it appeal so much is partly its resonance – the words once committed to memory are not easily forgotten. I sometimes use it as a vestry prayer before the main Sunday eucharist, surely a 'great matter' if ever there was one.

The real force of it, however, lies in the closing line. We trundle along, as we so often do in prayer, asking God to give us this, begging him to do that, longing to become the other. In this case, we ask for nothing more complicated than the grace to finish what we've started – though God knows many a leader may pray Drake's words in desperation at certain characters who promise to see to every outstanding task, and then neglect them all.

Often a prayer ends, 'through Jesus Christ our Lord', to prompt the faithful to agree to the petition to God the Father, through the Son, by saying 'Amen'. Here, though, we get instead words of stronger impact and sterner challenge – Jesus becomes the one 'that for the finishing of thy work laid down his life'. Suddenly we remember, amid the everyday business of church life and Christian faith, that discipleship may cost us little, or may cost us everything.

When we meet people who are driven by their faith, it can be an uncomfortable experience. Like the saints of old, they intimidate us with their certainty, and overwhelm us with their convictions. But we recognize, even in that off-putting single-mindedness, a kinship with the purity of intention of Jesus himself. His oneness with the Father was uncluttered by the personal baggage and axes-to-grind that motivate either our certainties or our prevaricating. He saw clearly the implications of obedience, and, in full knowledge, accepted them.

That connection between accepting a burden and the challenge of how we may be called to lay it down is not easily forgotten. The next time we hear Drake's prayer, we might pay better attention to its beginning: how easily a reviser could have simplified it to 'O God, when your servants begin any major project'. But, no, the words, precise and insistent – 'when thou givest' – bid us beware of forgetting that every impulse for his glory comes from God, and not from us.

Cally Hammond

Growing in love

Lord God,
make my legs move ever faster . . .
and my path true to your will.
Give me a heart never short of energy . . .
and growing in love for those around me.
As I strive for success,
teach me the secret of godly contentment.

Richard Nerurkar, marathon runner

Like Richard Nerurkar, I am a marathon runner. He was the most successful British male marathon runner of the 1990s, coming fifth in the 1996 Olympics. His personal best time was two hours, eight minutes and 36 seconds in the 1997 London Marathon.

I have completed one London Marathon, and am still dining out on the achievement. It took me a whole five hours and 13 minutes (seconds don't matter, believe me), but I like to think that Mr Nerurkar and I have something in common. We trained, we strove, and we ran.

When athletes are in training, muscles are honed and stretched, techniques polished, and minds become focused. Each athlete, from gymnasts to rowers, from javelin-throwers to swimmers, will be seeking perfection in body and mind. Each one will be chasing a medal, a personal best, the perfect score. And we, the armchair athletes of the nation, cheer them on, and groan when they fail.

This prayer reminds us that personal achievement has its place, and that striving for success is human. But 'success' means different things to different people. The international athlete wants to win her gold. The celebrated pianist wants to play the greatest Beethoven of his generation. The teenager wants to get good grades in exams. The elderly man is aiming to walk to the Post Office and back without getting out of breath.

When I worked in a school for children with special needs, I encountered a very disabled six-year-old boy. One day, he said the word 'Yeah' to me. This might not sound much compared with the wide vocabulary of many children his age, but when I told the class teacher about it, we celebrated this enormous achievement with as much joy as if he'd scored a goal for England. What counts as 'success' depends on the point from which you start.

Whatever our own successes might be, and however humble our strivings, this prayer reminds us that those strivings are part of who we are, and how God has made us. It is good to push ourselves.

The prayer is also honest in acknowledging limitations. Sometimes we falter in our endeavours, and call out to God for help: 'Lord,' says the runner, 'make my legs move ever faster . . .' Whatever we are aiming for – gold medals, promotion at work, acknowledgement for our efforts, a whole day without a cigarette – we can pray for a little help from God.

Richard Nerurkar is also a committed Christian, and in his prayer he puts our strivings into a wider context: we are called to love and serve God. Running is important to him, but of greater importance ultimately is his faith. It is his faith that will sustain him when he fails to achieve his goals and when his running career is over. Personal bests and medals on the mantelpiece will not give him the contentment he seeks. Only faith in God can do that.

The prayer celebrates our human striving, and acknowledges our need for help, but, in the end, it gently reminds us that we are called to something beyond achievement, however gratifying achievement might be: we are called to a faith that is contentment, a faith where all our strivings cease.

Whatever our own hopes, whatever we strive for, it is in God and not in our own strength that we find our fulfilment.

Georgina Byrne

Holy powers

I bind unto myself the power
Of the great love of Cherubim;
The sweet 'Well done' in judgement hour;
The service of the Seraphim,
Confessors' faith, Apostles' word,
The Patriarchs' prayers, the Prophets' scrolls,
All good deeds done unto the Lord,
And purity of virgin souls.
Against the demon snares of sin,
The vice that gives temptation force,
The natural lusts that war within,
The hostile men that mar my course;
Or few or many, far or nigh,
In every place, and in all hours,
Against their fierce hostility,
I bind to me these holy powers.

St Patrick's Breastplate (ascribed to St Patrick, 372–466,
translated by Mrs C. F. Alexander)

I bind to myself. I take responsibility for myself – first person singular. But I do so in solidarity with a vast community of obedience and commitment. The *Breastplate* is all about companionship.

The saints are with us; and these are not only the ones who name the name of Christ: their list includes the patriarchs and prophets who were obedient to God's will before Christ; we honour them in company with our old cousins the Jews, and with those other children of Abraham, the Muslims. There are good deeds done in even wider circles.

One of the most memorable people I have known was a woman of about my age, a Jew from central Europe. She had known the horrors of her people's experience under Nazism. She had nursed in India. She had survived the Mau Mau terrors of East Africa. She had pioneered a new form of pastoral ministry in an English university.

With this wide experience, she came to us in South Africa, to dedicate herself to the struggle against racism, injustice and poverty. With great vitality and generous humour, she gained the trust of all kinds of people. She was a breath of fresh air in a discouraging scene.

After only a few months, in her forties, she was diagnosed with incurable cancer. She had to leave South Africa and go to London. Soon after, my family and I also found ourselves as exiles in London. For all of us, it was a painful question: had we got it all wrong? What was the purpose?

As death approached, she felt and looked very depressed. Then she was given a vision. Thousands of people who had suffered through the pogroms, through Mau Mau, through racial oppression, were beckoning to her from 'the other side'; they were putting their reserves of courage, their accumulated credit of faith, at her disposal. With all this on her side, she won. She died looking and sounding like her old self.

In the Middle Ages, they called this idea the Treasury of Merit. She had found it for real. But it is what we celebrate at every eucharist. George MacLeod, founder of the Iona Community, used to say that Iona is 'a thin place', a place where the boundary between earth and heaven is transparent. Every Christian altar is a thin place, where we meet the angels and archangels and all the company of heaven.

In this faith, we can reckon with the enemy. Two more verses of the *Breastplate* follow this one; they are optional in the older books and omitted in the new. But without these verses, the *Breastplate* is like a kitchen without a sink – it may look more hygienic, but it won't have the equipment to deal with disorder and defilement.

Within the good creation, things go wrong in three ways, two of which we recognize in this verse. First, there are the contradictions within myself, the motives that St Paul describes so graphically as the evil that I do that I do not want to do.

A slight pressure on a brake pedal is boosted by the servo mechanism to become a force that can cause a heavy vehicle to stop. 'The vice that gives temptation force' works in a similar way. The energy from within me turns a little suggestion from outside into a commitment of sin. So I claim the powers of the Creator's success to obstruct this process.

Then there are the forces of evil, which come at me through people. I need to be realistic about them. If I am to love my enemies, I first need to acknowledge that that is what they are. Faced, for instance, with officers of the South African security police, it would be foolish to pretend that they are anything other than 'hostile men'. They certainly marred my course. One police captain gave me a wretched time in repeated interrogations, but gave far worse to others, especially black Africans. I claim the protection of divine power against the likes of him.

Then my wife notices that he wears a wedding ring. Somewhere out there, there is a woman who finds him a delight: unimaginable! But this helps us to recognize that he is also a victim of a system that he cannot either create or destroy. We wrestle not against flesh and blood . . . I claim the power of justice on the police captain's behalf, as well as my own.

John D. Davies

Nunc dimittis

Lord, now lettest thou thy servant depart in peace:
according to thy word.
For mine eyes have seen: thy salvation;
Which thou hast prepared: before the face of all people;
To be a light to lighten the Gentiles:
and to be the glory of thy people Israel.

Book of Common Prayer (Luke 2.29–32)

When my elder daughter was a baby, we took her to see her great-grandmother, who was over 90. The sight of one beginning her journey in the world cradled by one who was soon to end it was deeply moving. Here, for a few moments, generations overlapped, as someone who had lived most of her life in the previous century (and millennium) greeted someone who would live in this one. The extremity of the age of one and the youth of the other symbolized the passing on of a torch.

The story of Jesus' meeting with Simeon and Anna in the temple (Luke 2.25–38) evokes a similar image. This moment was marked not only by overlapping generations, centuries and millennia, but also by a change in the whole history of salvation: as Simeon proclaimed, he had seen God's salvation, for which he had waited for the whole of his life.

We do not know what Anna said (though there seems to have been a great deal of it, since she spoke 'about the child to all who were looking for the redemption of Jerusalem', Luke 2.38). In the moment when Simeon cradled this tiny baby, he recognized the shift that was taking place from the old to the new, and expressed it in the timeless words of the Nunc dimittis.

The amazing thing about Simeon was the humility with which he greeted Jesus. He knew that he had seen 'salvation', and that, for him, was enough. He accepted with equal tranquillity what Jesus brought, and the fact that he would not be around to see it. His words indicate that he knew that this moment in which he embraced the infant Jesus was the beginning of the end for him.

Though the translation in the Book of Common Prayer is the most beautiful rendition of the Nunc dimittis, it does not give full force to the present tense of the verb 'you are liberating (or releasing) your servant'.

Even as he held Jesus, Simeon knew that it marked an ending as well as a beginning. Most of us would find this knowledge unsettling or threatening, but Simeon apparently embraces it with joy because, in it, he has found peace and wholeness.

As we pray these words of Simeon, we can, if we choose, bind to ourselves his remarkable attitude to the chaotic change that God's kingdom brings with it: an attitude that greets and embraces the sweeping away of the world that we know, and that risks an unknown future with God.

We, like Simeon, can find freedom and peace in the unsettling and disturbing salvation of God. The Nunc dimittis signals the passing of a torch from Simeon to Jesus, and, if we choose, to us. The challenge it poses is whether, like Simeon, we can embrace the change that it brings.

Paula Gooder

Death

The gate of heaven

Bring us, O Lord God, at our last awakening
into the house and gate of heaven,
to enter into that gate and dwell in that house
where shall be no darkness nor dazzling,
but one equal light;
no noise nor silence, but one equal music;
no fears nor hopes, but one equal possession;
no ends nor beginnings,
but one equal eternity;
in the habitations of thy glory and dominion,
world without end. Amen.

John Donne (c.1572–1631)

I love this prayer, and often use it at funerals and memorial services. It is the sort of prayer that I want to use at the end of a busy day, during evensong, as the light is slanting across the quire, and there is that moment of pause as the business of the day is wrapped away into God. But it contains surprises.

John Donne did not originally write these words as a prayer. They were first part of a sermon he preached in 1628 about Jacob's dream, and were lifted and given prayer form in the twentieth century by Eric Milner-White, Dean of York Minster.

All the words are Donne's, and when I pray the prayer I often think of him, with his rackety life – his adventures on the high seas, his secret marriage and disgrace, his ambition, and his eventual arrival at the Deanery of St Paul's. All this reminds me that he was like many modern men and women, with an enormous number of ups and downs, and short careers in this and that or nothing.

This prayer is remarkable. It's remarkable that John Donne could have written it – was it, I wonder, because he led a rackety life that he could see through to the beauty and serenity of the life of God in such a way?

Perhaps we would believe more intensely if our lives had more ups and downs; or perhaps rackety people have more to offer us than we recognize.

Yet the prayer is also remarkable because it speaks of the life of God as being somehow different from either extreme of human experience. God is not an excess of light, a dazzling, nor an excess of darkness. He is 'one equal light', a different kind of light entirely. Nor is he simply to be found in an excess of music, rather like a continuous 'Hallelujah Chorus', nor even, simply, in silence. There is a different quality about God, well expressed by those repeated phrases: 'one equal music', 'one equal possession', 'one equal eternity'.

And I find that consoling. It mends all my fractures at the ends of things. I know that my music often moves into unmusic; my light becomes darkness, and then light again. But, when all is said and done, God's life is such that it will repair all that I might suffer.

God is not simply more of the same. He is not the height of ecstasy nor even the end of ecstasy. He comes from a different place. He completes and transforms all that we lack and all that we have. He is a trumpet call from across the boundary.

Melvyn Matthews

Mourners' Kaddish

Magnified and sanctified be God's great name
throughout the world which he has created according to his will.
May he establish his kingdom in your lifetime and in your days,
and within the lifetime of the whole house of Israel,
speedily and soon; and say, Amen.
May his great name be blessed forever and to all eternity.
Blessed and praised, glorified and exalted,
extolled and honoured, magnified and lauded be the name of the Holy
  One,
blessed be he, beyond all the blessings and hymns,
praises and consolations which are uttered in the world; and say, Amen.
Let the name of the Lord be blessed from this time forth and for ever-
  more.
May there be abundant peace from heaven,
and life for us and for all Israel; and say, Amen.
My help is from the Lord, who made heaven and earth.
He who makes peace in his high places,
may he make peace for us and for all Israel; and say, Amen.

Traditional

Jewish law requires that a son pray the mourners' *Kaddish* for 11 months
after the death of a parent. Daughters often keep the same custom,
though they are not required to do so. Afterwards, it is said annually on
the anniversary. It must be prayed publicly, which means in the company
of at least ten adult males. All the mourners present pray the *Kaddish*
together, and the whole congregation makes the responses.

Yet the *Kaddish* is not about death. Its theme is the greatness of God,
and it asks for the coming of his kingdom, and for peace. Nor is *Kaddish*
exclusively a mourners' prayer. It developed first as an acclamation after
the reading or interpretation of God's holy law; the same prayer, with
slight variations, is used at various points in the service.

The mourners' *Kaddish* has its special place in the public liturgy. Many
rabbis have pointed out that it is not a prayer that requests heavenly
blessing for the dead person; rather, the act of praying it according to

custom demonstrates why the parent deserves such a blessing – namely, that he taught his son to honour God before the congregation.

In terms of content, it is not a difficult prayer for a Christian to pray – the words and images are all familiar; to speak of God's people Israel has been for centuries also to speak of the Church. But why would we wish to pray it?

We might use it as it was originally used – a prayer of adoration and wonder at the greatness of God; an expression of faith and trust. We might value it as a prayer – one of many – that we share with Jewish brothers and sisters, and as an expression of unity between two peoples of the book.

As the rabbis have said, it includes our shortest and most often repeated prayer, 'Amen', which is prayed by Jew, Christian and Muslim alike. Not a word to be neglected, certainly: in the largest synagogues, a flag was waved from a platform at the appropriate moment, to ensure that all the worshippers joined in the Amen together.

We might also find it helpful to use it as a Jewish mourner does – to mark the death of someone close. Our own liturgy does not offer an equivalent formal context for sorrow, or a way of giving structure and expression to the process of grieving. Leon Wieseltier has written in depth of how he felt duty-bound to recite *Kaddish* three times a day during his year of mourning his father – though he was not a devout or even an observant Jew at the time (*Kaddish*, Picador, 1998). This helped him to come to terms with his bereavement, and to explore his feelings, through the medium of a tradition he had previously scarcely acknowledged: 'The *Kaddish* is my good fortune. It looks after the externalities, and so saves me from improvising the rituals of my bereavement.'

What comfort does the mourners' *Kaddish* offer a bereaved person? Partly the comfort of doing something. Our instinct to give, and to sacrifice at such times is strong. The sacrifice and offering involved in a commitment to pray *Kaddish* is in tune with our deepest spiritual instincts.

There is also the sense of setting death in its proper context, one of 'no ends, nor beginnings, but one equal eternity'. John Donne's prayer reflects much the same instinct. Every natural disaster and every man-made catastrophe, just like every peaceful individual death in due time, draws the believer into remembering that 'we brought nothing into the world, and it is certain we can carry nothing out.' When we are given to life, and when we are taken by death, we are the Lord's.

Cally Hammond

Russian Contakion of the Departed

Give rest, O Christ, to thy servant with thy saints:
where sorrow and pain are no more;
neither sighing but life everlasting.
Thou only art immortal,
the Creator and Maker of man:
And we are mortal, formed of the earth,
and unto earth shall we return:
For so thou didst ordain,
when thou createdst me, saying,
Dust thou art, and unto dust shalt thou return.
All we go down to the dust, and weeping
o'er the grave we make our song:
Alleluya, alleluya, alleluya.
Give rest, O Christ, to thy servant with thy saints:
where sorrow and pain are no more;
neither sighing but life everlasting.

The *Contakion* is a special form of hymn used in the liturgies of the Eastern Church. It has become familiar to Anglicans through its inclusion in the *English Hymnal* (no. 744), where the words are set to an evocative arrangement of the Russian chant by Sir Walter Parratt.

Prayer for the dead might well be called a natural instinct seeking a theology. From the age of the Fathers, Christians have felt the need to commend to God those who have died in the faith of Christ, and have felt it fitting to make that commendation at the celebration of the eucharist.

St Augustine records in his *Confessions* the dying words of his mother St Monica: 'All I ask of you is that wherever you may be, you will always remember me at the altar of God.' This instinct came to express itself both in the magnificent spiritual edifice of Dante's *Purgatorio*, and in the degenerate customs that led the reformers to exclude any explicit prayer for the dead from the Prayer Book.

The editors of the *English Hymnal* were astute in choosing an Orthodox prayer for the departed, and so getting behind the Reformation controversies. The emphasis here is on Christian joy in the face of death, not on purgation or punishment. Only God is immortal, and our mortality is an unavoidable part of our fallen humanity.

Yet, as we weep over the grave where we return to the dust from which we were made, we sing Alleluya, the song of the resurrection. From Christ we receive life everlasting, and our prayer for the departed is that they may be at rest with his saints, for whom sorrow and pain are no more.

When I hear this prayer sung at the eucharist, it makes a vivid appeal to the imagination: the haunting chant recalls the atmosphere of devotion that Nicolai Leskov portrays so wonderfully in his novels about Russian parish life. In doing so, it evokes a picture of the universality of the Church of God: so many different Christians through the ages gathered at the eucharist, both those who have left behind them the memory of heroic virtue, and those, like Chione, an otherwise unknown woman from Asia Minor mentioned by Dom Gregory Dix. Her humble fourth-century tombstone says only that she 'had found Jerusalem for she prayed much'.

Every year I attend the annual requiem of the Guild of All Souls. As we celebrate the eucharist, the dead seem very close: members of my family, priests who have taught me the faith, parishioners, friends and benefactors. One day, I will be prayed for at that mass among the faithful departed, and I will know that the bond of charity that unites us in Christ remains unbroken, even in death.

Robin Ward

A song

Lord, when the sense of thy sweet grace
Sends up my soul to seek thy face.
Thy blessed eyes breed such desire,
I dy in love's delicious Fire.
  O love, I am thy Sacrifice.
Be still triumphant, blessed eyes.
Still shine on me, fair suns! that I
Still may behold, though still I dy.

Richard Crashaw (1612–49)

Death is not a topic of fashionable conversation. Modern western culture appears to be obsessed with prolonging life and youth at all costs. Perhaps only history will judge whether luxuries such as cosmetic surgery contribute to or diminish the hope of ultimate flourishing. Our ancestors had to make do with prayers for a 'good death', and the verbal, visual and liturgical forms of *memento mori*.

Richard Crashaw was a poet influenced by the devotional writing of late-medieval England, and by the ecstatic, white-hot poetry of the European Counter-Reformation. Entranced by the effervescent holiness of God, the believer is able to approach God only through the veils of prayer, tears, contemplative vigil, or the action of the liturgy.

As was true of many of his literary contemporaries, 'dying' for Crashaw was about fulfilment rather than stagnation. To die is to lift the veil – or rather, to have the veil lifted. In this prayer, it is the grace of God that stirs the believer to enter into that most awesome search: to see the face of God.

Our desire for God, which has its origin in God's desire for us, is met by the generous gaze of God, which feeds our yearning for holiness and wholeness. This points towards the final consummation of the inner life of prayer, so much so that the one who is caught up in this seeking becomes the sacrifice of love.

But, within the Christian tradition, sacrifice is for consummation, not annihilation. We do not lose our identity in the face of God: rather, we experience the fullness of that identity, and begin to understand the dynamic ramifications of God's love for us in the 'delicious fire' of his gaze. To 'dy in love's delicious Fire' is a communicative action, a response to God's grace. Here, sacrifice is a form of giving back, so that through the action of God's perpetual generosity we can receive more. Notably, the only features of the divine face singled out by Crashaw are those 'blessed eyes'. When we pause to look into someone's eyes properly, we can experience a two-fold exchange, a communication that surpasses words – a mutual knowing that goes beyond a verbal message.

As we look into those 'blessed eyes', we begin the cycle of searching more intensely, until we finally experience the full lifting of the veil in our physical death. In our day-to-day prayer lives, this is not always a comfortable or comforting reality. Looking into those eyes may sometimes seem disorienting, as we begin to understand more about God, and therefore more about ourselves.

Rowan Williams has likened being held close to the breast of God to the experience of lovers kissing. On the one hand, it is hard to see the lover while kissing; on the other hand, one has the best possible view.

Kissing can be clumsy, and often opens up a road that has few signposts, and no predetermined end. The slow journey of learning how you can be still, as yourself, in God's consuming but generative gaze, shares similar characteristics. As we learn to see the other fully, such intense experiences sometimes re-order the contours of our lives.

Crashaw prays that God's blessed eyes be 'triumphant', even in our weaknesses: to shine on us still, that as we glimpse God's glory and the ramifications of his love for us in our prayer, we may 'dy' a little more, as we continue on the pilgrimage to our final death. Then, as the writer of 1 John has it, we shall see him as he is. If that's truly the final consummation, perhaps the twenty-first century could do with more *memento mori*.

Jamie Hawkey

A bed of hope

O living God, in Jesus Christ
you were laid in the tomb
at this evening hour,
and so sanctified the grave
to be a bed of hope to your people.
Give us courage and faith
to die daily to our sin and pride,
that even as this flesh and blood decays,
our lives may still grow in you,
that at our last day
our dying may be done so well
that we live in you for ever. Amen.

Jim Cotter, from *Prayer at Night*

Jesus is taken down from the cross and laid in the tomb: the helpless Saviour; utter powerlessness. Set alongside it is our confrontation with the horror and inevitability of our own death. These two awesome objects of contemplation are united – comprehended – in the gentle experience of 'this evening hour'. Christ's tomb and our own grave are both viewed through the prism of tonight's bed. Thus that which our imagination can hardly encompass (the deposition), and that which our courage can seldom face (our own death) are made tractable through that which our bodies know deeply – the sense of nocturnal rest.

Jim Cotter has taken one of the final prayers from compline, and added three new dimensions. One is the anticipation of death in the treatment of our own sin ('die daily'). Another is the engaging contrast between the decay of the physical body and the growth of the spiritual one. The last is the notion of a good death.

I buried a member of our congregation recently. She had told me of the things that meant most to her – family, music, work, garden, faith. A couple of months later, we spoke again. If she had only a few weeks, what were the key things she wanted to do, to say, to complete? She pondered, and planned. I know that the things she decided on that day, God gave her time to say and do.

The next month, she asked me to spend some time with her as she let go of the one or two things that still lay uneasy on her heart. Together we allowed God to release her from the burden of them. Three days before she died, we prayed together, and I commended each part of her life, body, mind and spirit, to the God who had made and so much cherished her. Finally, shortly after her death, I had the opportunity to sit with others beside her body and recognize before God everything that had happened. Afterwards, there was only one word spoken, and that word was 'beautiful'.

She instinctively knew what this prayer articulates: that holiness is the opening of the heart to embrace what God is doing in one's life; that devotion is about seeing the eternal in the everyday; and that ministry is about the power one is given when one is given mundane ways of encountering the unfathomable.

I remember hearing an angry young man say, 'The Church is good with death; it's just life it hasn't yet come to terms with.' For years, I remembered this as a searing criticism. Now I'm not so sure. To die well: is this not perhaps the greatest gift we can give to our community? To look into the face of death and see only the compassionate, merciful face of Christ: is this not the greatest witness of all?

Sam Wells

Hope

Christk the morning star

Christ is the morning star
who, when the night of this world is past,
brings to his saints
the promise of the light of life
and opens everlasting day.

The Venerable Bede (673–735)

Is this a prayer? Perhaps technically it's not, because it isn't addressed to God. But, if prayer is the vehicle through which we come closer to the beauty of God, then these sublime words of the Venerable Bede must certainly count as true prayer. The words are to be found behind Bede's tomb in the Galilee Chapel of Durham Cathedral, written in a script that is both wonderful and hard to decipher.

Yet that seems strangely appropriate for the humble monk of Wearmouth-Jarrow, the quiet scholar who hardly ever left the monastery, but who was at the same time an astounding influence in the dark years between the decline of Rome and the flowering of the Middle Ages. It's not far off the mark to say that the intellectual life of Europe looked to the light that burned in this distant Northumbrian monastery.

I have stood to preside and preach in that monastery chapel (now St Paul's) in Jarrow, where the consecration inscription marks the date as 685. I have felt the ancient strength of that scholar's faith. The light of his Lord shone in the darkness, and the darkness has never – and could never – put it out.

So the image of light that suffuses this prayer speaks vividly of both the author of the prayer and the author of the light. The metaphor of Christ as the morning star is timeless and evocative. So often, we struggle through the 'night of this world', in whatever shape it takes for us, and we long for a sign of hope, a promise of a future. In the resurrection of Christ, we have the first intimation that dawn is on its way.

When the night is past, like the dove bringing the olive leaf back to the ark, Christ brings a promise. That promise is of the light of life, the jubilant colour and extravagance of life 'dipped in God', as D. H. Lawrence puts it.

Not content with that transforming gift, Christ our morning star goes on throwing open the shutters, so that we begin to grasp the true end of this light, which is the everlasting day where 'they will not need the light of a lamp or the light of the sun for the Lord God will give them light' (Revelation 22.5). Thus the first glimmering star gives way to the light of life as God intends it, and then to the fullness of God's eternal presence.

This is the light that illuminated Bede's steady scholarship and disciplined holiness. This is the light that stops people in their tracks as they pass the tomb of Bede in that glorious chapel. And this is the light that I trust will surround my daughter and son-in-law in their marriage, as they made their vows alongside Bede's tomb in that same chapel.

John Pritchard

Green and growing hope

Creator God,
Give us a heart for simple things:
    love and laughter,
    bread and wine,
    tales and dreams.
Fill our lives
with green and growing hope;
make us a people of justice
whose song is Alleluia
and whose name breathes love.

Anonymous, South Africa

I have reason to be grateful to Africa. Both our daughters found their faith renewed by exposure to the vitality and the questions of that great continent. So I'm drawn to a prayer that comes out of that rich Christian environment.

I'm also drawn to language that offers colour, texture and evocative images. Prayer functions best in that mode, I believe – allusive and translucent, drawing us into engagement and response. And I have to admit to being a sucker for anything that talks about simplicity. As my life becomes more and more complex, I respond immediately to the image of 'simple things' – 'love and laughter, bread and wine, tales and dreams'.

Love and laughter are wonderful companions, and if we were able to exhibit more of them in the Church, it would be deeply attractive to others. Tales and dreams lock into the deepest strata of our experience, and we in the Church have superb tales to tell. Bread and wine are placed at the heart of the list, in the centre of human life, where they belong.

Just when I want to linger over those six gifts for which we pray, we're swept on to another set of images. The idea of being full of 'green and growing hope' brings a smile of expectation. Here is a living image from a country where the journey of hope has been a rollercoaster for many years, but the picture of natural, steady growth, of the inexorable rise of inexhaustible hope, is one I can embrace with delight.

Rightly in a continent such as Africa, issues of justice are a central concern of prayer. 'Make us a people of justice' isn't just asking God to apply a magician's art; it's asking that we will have characters that are just, so that just actions may flow from just instincts – a much more demanding request. To have a just character requires constant exposure to the message of the prophets and the life of Jesus, and a constant realignment of our devious tendency to self-seeking. When we ask for a just character, we ask a great deal.

But a people of justice will find themselves singing Alleluia because they know their alignments are true. The Truth and Reconciliation Commission headed by Archbishop Desmond Tutu recognized that truth has to be named, but retribution has to be resisted. That's justice at a deeper level than we usually manage. It's where this prayer comes from.

So we pray that we'll find ourselves singing Alleluia and having a name that 'breathes love'. That's a lovely vision, and not one we have deserved over recent periods of ecclesiastical controversy. Would that the world instinctively associated the Church with love, generosity and compassion. If that sounds unlikely, then pray for it.

John Pritchard

Purge our eyes

Lord, purge our eyes to see
Within the seed a tree,
Within the glowing egg a bird,
Within the shroud a butterfly.
Till, taught by such we see
Beyond all creatures, thee
And hearken to thy tender word
And hear its 'Fear not; it is I.'

Christina Rossetti (1830–94)

For many of us, there exists a tension between the people we are, and who we might be; between the reality of the lives we live, and those to which we aspire. Christina Rossetti, the Pre-Raphaelite English poet, led a life of restraint, hampered by ill health, abandoned love affairs, and possibly even by her own religiosity. Nevertheless, she was a woman who was able to express feelings of love and heartbreak with eloquence and passion, as evidenced by her writing. This creative energy found an outlet in her poetry and prayers.

This prayer, perhaps reflecting her internal struggles, recognizes the promise inherent in all creation. Like a guided meditation, it focuses our attention on life in its embryonic stage – when it is still contained and yet to break out. Then the moment comes: the seed splits open, the egg cracks or the chrysalis sheds its casing, and emergent life bursts out, free to be and to become.

This is the beginning of a life cycle that puts us in touch with the mind of God. Each living thing points beyond itself to the creator, through whom the world came into being, and in whose image we are made – the created world being an expression of the divine, in which we encounter the risen Christ, the 'I' referred to at the end of the prayer.

As Christ burst from the tomb on Easter morning, so nature is irrepressible. Death gives way to life. The divine story of death and resurrection is constantly played out in the world around us. Yet this prayer reminds us that we fail to appreciate what it is we behold. 'Purge our eyes to see . . .' suggests that our vision is clouded.

Before we can recognize properly the treasure contained within the

{ 176 }

outer shell, we need to rid ourselves of whatever prevents us from seeing clearly – whether it is lack of imagination, ignorance, or the fear to which Rossetti alludes. When asked to contemplate nature's hidden secrets, we are challenged to face the unknown, to reach out to the indefinable 'I AM' revealed to Moses in the burning bush. This is the God of surprises, whom death could not contain.

Life cannot be contained. Our two young children remind me of this every day, as their two distinct personalities develop. For me, this prayer is a reminder of the need to let them go; to let them find their wings and fly. But, more importantly, the images of expectant life are a reminder of all children's intrinsic worth, irrespective of whether or not their potential is realized.

In the same way, when I pray this prayer in relationship to my mother, who has Alzheimer's and has retreated into a world I can no longer reach, it brings me up short. Those of us who may doubt the value of such lives may be reminded by this prayer's words and images of the hidden worth of people who struggle to communicate, and the intimacy with which they are connected to their maker. Therein lies the power of this prayer.

Annabel Shilson-Thomas

A promise in suffering

Lord: help us to see in the groaning of creation
not death throes, but birth pangs;
help us to see in suffering a promise for the future,
because it is a cry against the inhumanity of the present.
Help us to glimpse in protest the dawn of justice,
in the Cross the pathway to resurrection,
and in sufferings the seeds of joy.

Rubem Alves, from *All Year Round*
(based on Romans 8.18–25)

This prayer has a directness that gives it energy, and a simplicity that be-lies its profundity. There is no soft-edged preamble, just an open request that goes straight to the point: 'Lord: help us'. Help us to hope when eve-rything militates against it. And why? Because hidden within destruction are the seeds of resurrection.

Here Rubem Alves offers us a reflection born out of suffering, not a simple statement of belief. His life among some of the poorest communi-ties in the world, the dispossessed of Brazil, means that he is better placed than most to question the misery of many people's lives. And that is why this prayer has such power. It is a reflection on reality. It speaks to our hearts, not just our heads.

Whether spoken by a community or an individual, the value of this prayer lies in its acknowledgement of pain and in its refusal to accept the injustice of suffering. Unlike so many anodyne prayers of the Church, which prefer reverence and passivity, it does not shy away from lan-guage that speaks of human agony – groaning, death throes, birth pangs, inhumanity, protest and suffering – and yet it is not a desolate prayer. Rather, it sees our longing for transformation as a sign of hope. Because we protest against the present, we have a vision of something better.

This call to engage with suffering is central to Christian tradition, and yet it is often neglected in our prayers. Very rarely do our prayers wrestle with God in the manner of Job, who demanded to know why the inno-cent should suffer, or challenge God, as Moses did when negotiating on his people's behalf. Very rarely do we allow ourselves to express anger, doubt or disbelief, like the psalmist, or, taking a leaf out of Jeremiah's book, to lament and protest in equal measure.

And yet, as this prayer suggests, it is when we are in the depths, groaning with creation, that we engage most profoundly with our maker; for we are stripped bare of all that protects us. Jesus' cry from the cross is 'against the inhumanity of the present'. 'My God, my God, why have you forsaken me,' often cited as evidencing separation from God, also offers us a place where God's protest against injustice meets our own. God engages with our suffering, and refuses to let it have the last word. Resurrection beckons, as does the dawn of justice.

Recalling the eschatological passage in Romans 8.18–25, which looks forward with eager expectation to the liberation of all creation and the freedom of the children of God, this prayer encourages us to a change of attitude. We are called from acceptance to challenge, from pessimism to optimism, from despair to hope – not through a denial of the present, but through glimpsing its future transformation.

For me, this position has integrity. It has an honesty that lets neither God nor us off the hook, which is one of the reasons it appeals to me. What I had not foreseen when I chose this prayer is how it might resonate with those watching with the dying. Seeing my mother's body protest as she took her last breaths, this prayer rang true in a way I had never expected.

Annabel Shilson-Thomas

God of changeable power

O God of unchangeable power and eternal light,
Look favourably upon thy whole Church,
That wonderful and sacred mystery;
And by the tranquil operation of thy perpetual providence
Carry out the work of man's salvation;
And let the whole world feel and see that things which were
    cast down are being raised up;
That those which had grown old are being made new;
And that all things are returning into unity
Through him by whom all things were made,
Even thy Son Jesus Christ our Lord. Amen.

Gelasian Sacramentary

This prayer comes from the collection of eighth-century liturgical texts known as the *Gelasian Sacramentary*, which reflect the way in which the rite of the Church of Rome was adapted for use in the kingdom of the Franks. It is the work of an unknown Christian praying in the very heart of the Dark Ages, when all the comforting landmarks inherited from the classical past seemed on the point of eclipse in the face of barbarism and war. Christians in similar circumstances have often found themselves drawn to a bleak, apocalyptic view of the world; this prayer is remarkable because of its optimism and confidence.

The prayer begins by invoking God as the source of unchanging power and eternal light. This is a scriptural theme, drawing on James 1.17: 'Every good endowment and every perfect gift is from above, coming down from the Father of lights with whom there is no variation or shadow due to change.' The prayer for God's favour is made on behalf of the Church, 'that wonderful and sacred mystery'. The grim realities of church life in the eighth century make our own disagreements and poor witness seem almost benign, but the writer sees not simply the Church militant in earth, but the saints triumphant in heaven, in whom the wonder and the holiness of the mystical Body of Christ are made clear.

The serene optimism of the prayer is never more apparent than in the commendation of the work of redemption to the 'tranquil operation' of God's 'perpetual providence'. This confidence in God expects to see that the working of divine providence will be felt and seen in the world. Bishop Hensley Henson wrote that 'the inadequacy of the practical effect of Christianity . . . has always seemed to me the most formidable difficulty in the way of discipleship.'

So much effort and activity, so many centuries of evangelization and devotion, seem to have had so little effect. The writer of this prayer recognizes the same difficulty, and looks forward to a visible restoration of all things in Christ, in which both the vision of the Old Testament prophets and the new Jerusalem of Revelation are fulfilled.

The philosopher Alistair MacIntyre concluded his book *After Virtue* (Duckworth, 1981) by saying that to survive the moral anarchy of the present we need a new St Benedict. It is inspiring to think of the Benedictines who preserved this prayer for posterity, surrounded by violence and decay, watching the last vestiges of humanity and civility fade from the life of their society, calmly and confidently persevering in the practice of their faith.

The prayer for the Church in the 1928 Prayer Book calls the saints 'lights of the world in their several generations'. When we celebrate All Saints' Day and All Souls' Day in November, we make the effort to think of the Church as a 'wonderful and sacred mystery', to be judged not simply by what we see of her on earth, but by the glory of her members in heaven.

Robin Ward

Advent and Christmas

Thy daily visitation

We beseech thee, O Lord,
to cleanse our minds by thy daily visitation;
that when thy Son, our Lord, cometh
he may find in us a mansion
prepared for himself.

Gelasian Sacramentary, from Evelyn Underhill,
Eucharistic Prayers from the Ancient Liturgies

The season of Advent is one of the loveliest of the Church's year. 'Lent without the penance' some have called it. The Advent sections in our hymnbooks contain more than their fair share of masterpieces. We revel in the ancient liturgical provision from the responsory 'I looked from afar' early on Advent Sunday morning to the Magnificat antiphons at evening prayer during the week before Christmas. The hymn 'O come, O come, Emmanuel' brings them all together.

The themes that underlie the Advent prayers, however, are not as cosy as we might imagine from this picture of liturgical contentment. Advent asks us to address the four last things: death, judgement, heaven and hell. It asks us to contemplate three comings of Christ: his coming at one particular place and time, his coming here and now, and his coming at the end of time. Advent asks us to think of Christ as king, as well as baby; as judge, as well as shepherd.

The *Gelasian Sacramentary*, from which this prayer comes, is one of the most important ancient liturgical manuscripts. Kept in the Vatican Library with a collection of other liturgical books that form a loose family, it seems to date from mid-eighth-century Paris. Its influence on the Western Church in the Middle Ages, and in turn on Cranmer when compiling the 1549 Prayer Book, was profound.

We hear an echo of this older prayer in the Prayer Book collect for Advent Sunday ('Almighty God, give us grace that we may cast away the works of darkness, and put upon us the armour of light . . .'). For centuries, this collect was part of the preparation for mass, and it still remains in use in some places as a prayer with servers or choir in the vestry. This translation is the work of Evelyn Underhill, who wrote prolifically and sensitively about the medieval mystical tradition until her death in 1941.

The first word to strike us from this collect is 'cleanse'. It is a particularly resonant liturgical word. In a prayer that Cranmer reused from the priest's private preparation before mass, we pray: 'Cleanse the thoughts of our hearts by the inspiration of thy Holy Spirit.' The current Roman Catholic office (in its Latin version) retains a preparatory prayer asking God to 'cleanse my heart from all vain, evil and wandering thoughts'.

More dramatic is the rite of blessing and sprinkling holy water at the start of the eucharist. The traditional chant for this sprinkling is still often heard: *Asperges me*, 'Thou shalt purge me, O Lord, with hyssop, and I shall be clean.'

A second word to strike us is 'daily'. Our liturgical preparation is aided in Advent by the lectionary. In particular, we hear the prophecy of Isaiah building up to Christmas night. These four weeks are a manageable period when we all should try to be at the altar and take seriously a programme of regular prayer.

Advent is a period of preparation to greet the Christ-child at his 'visitation' on Christmas night, at every moment of our Christian lives, and at the end of time. One day, we will all have to give an account of how we followed our God-given vocation. Priests will have to give an account of their pastoral care; parents of how they attempted to bring up their children; teachers of how they helped their pupils; and so on. It is a sobering thought.

Christ will come as judge. He is our shepherd, brother and friend, but he remains our judge, however merciful. The best Advent preparation of all is to acknowledge that fact, use the simple but difficult words 'have mercy on me, a sinner', and rejoice in the forgiveness he brings.

Kenneth Macnab

Zealous apostle

O glorious St John the Baptist, most zealous apostle,
who, without working any miracle on others
   but solely by the example of thy life of penance
   and the power of thy word,
didst draw after thee the multitudes,
in order to dispose them to receive the Messiah worthily,
and to listen to his heavenly doctrine:
pray that it may be given unto us,
by means of an example of a holy life and the exercise
   of every good work,
to bring many souls to God.

Prayer 457, the *Raccolta* (1950) (adapted)

This prayer shows us another human figure who dominates Advent litur-gies: John the Baptist. Yet, unlike Joseph and Mary, John did not take part in the story of the last few weeks, days and hours before the birth of Christ on Christmas night. At the time of the drama in Bethlehem, John was in his own crib, looking up at the face of his mother Elizabeth.

In the story of the visitation, John, even in the womb, recognizes Christ. With the little kick he gives Elizabeth, he seems to say: 'Behold the Lamb of God,' words he will use explicitly many years later (John 1.29). Renais-sance painters were very fond of painting the Holy Family with St John the Baptist. Very often, the two cherubic children, Jesus and John, can be distinguished by the ribbon John holds bearing those words.

How will a child grow up? In John's case, the chubby little boy of the paintings turned into a striking, if not alarming, figure. His appear-ance, his diet and his message are all disturbing. In the first few verses of Mark's Gospel, he emerges from the desert, a lone figure, with a dramatic and urgent message: 'a baptism of repentance for the forgiveness of sins' (Mark 1.4).

This prayer, which originated in Italy, is found in the official Roman Catholic collection of prayers known as the *Raccolta* (the word means 'collection' in Italian), which has been through several editions since its first publication in Rome in 1807. This version is adapted from an Amer-ican edition published in the 1950s.

The prayer brings home to us quite how different the story of John the

Baptist is from that of the bulk of New Testament saints. St Peter, for example, performed healing miracles (Acts 5.15). St Paul escaped from prison by a miraculous intervention (Acts 16.26). The grace of being a miracle-worker was not given to John. His time in prison ended not with escape, but with a savage death.

At the same time, the prayer reminds us that there was more to John's ministry than the power of persuasive oratory. True, he must have preached with urgency and conviction, but we may assume that the large numbers who followed him did so as much through his example as his message.

This chimes with our experience. How many people are talked into a relationship with Jesus? How many see something of Jesus in the lives and example of other people? Was the principal influence on your faith something someone said, or did, or simply something he or she was? The prayer reminds us that we are all missionaries.

John is an odd man out. He stands at the end of the long line of Old Testament figures, and yet he denies he is a prophet. He is the greatest born of women, says Jesus, and yet he is less than so many others. Even as he lay in jail, his words were coming true: 'He [Jesus] must increase, but I must decrease' (John 3.30).

Some churches, such as the chapel of Pusey House in Oxford, make this point in stone. The roof bosses in the nave bear the names of the Old Testament prophets. As the chancel vaulting sweeps towards the high altar, we find the names of the evangelists and apostles. John's roof-boss stands over the choir screen, at a half-way house, neither one thing nor the other.

John continues to speak to us, pointing towards Christ and insisting: 'Behold the Lamb of God.'

Kenneth Macnab

Virgin of virgins

O Virgin of virgins, how shall this be?
For neither before thee was any like thee, nor shall
  there be after.
Daughters of Jerusalem, why marvel ye at me?
The thing which ye behold is a divine mystery.

Medieval English antiphon for 23 December,
English Hymnal, no. 734; *New English Hymnal*, no. 503

Matthew and Luke give us no words from Mary's lips as they describe the intimate scene on Christmas night. Luke, however, gives us plenty of words from an earlier scene.

At the annunciation, Mary's response to Gabriel had been one of amazement, wonder, puzzlement, bravery, faithfulness and trust. 'Let it be done to me according to thy word.' For most of Christian history, her Magnificat has been recited every night. Every night it has something new to tell us. From the moment of her overshadowing by the Spirit, we are led on to the scene we celebrate now, nine months later.

The mysterious entry 'O Sapientia' in the calendar of the Book of Common Prayer for 16 December is one of the many survivals from the medieval sources on which Cranmer drew. It refers to the antiphons sung before and after the Magnificat during the final week of Advent, as the liturgy draws us on, ever faster, our feet stumbling, as it were, with the shepherds' on their way to the stable.

Each night, Christ is addressed with a ringing 'O' and an Old Testament title. Each antiphon ends with an equally ringing 'Come.' In the eighteenth century, they were woven into a Latin hymn, which entered our hymnbooks a century later as 'O come, O come, Emmanuel'.

The Prayer Book is a day out of step with most calendars. This is because medieval England added this extra antiphon for the night before Christmas Eve. There were several local variations across Europe. The *English Hymnal* printed the antiphons in full, and the *New English Hymnal* provided the plainchant melodies.

Having addressed Christ for a week, we now look at his mother.

Neither before nor since has any human been called in the way that she was. God the Son entered our world in one particular womb – hers. He was born on one particular night, and in one particular place. Only one human being was chosen and prepared for this task. Short of the Second Coming, hers is a unique calling.

Yet Mary is one of us and for all of us. She shows us what it is to be redeemed. Christ, her Saviour and ours, cannot do that. He enters heaven as the Redeemer. Alongside the other things we learn from her 'Yes' to God, Mary shows us the common heavenly destiny of the redeemed.

Bishop Humphry Beevor (a former editor of the *Church Times*) meditated famously on the scene in an Advent sermon.

The first thing a child sees when he looks up into his mother's eyes is the reflection of his own face in them. I like to think that was the first thing that the Baby Jesus saw at his birth, the first recollection of his life – his own face, shining, reflected in his mother's eyes. . . May he see that reflection in your soul and mine when we meet him in our communions on Christmas Day. (*Catholic Sermons*, SPCK, 1932)

Kenneth Macnab

A divine generation

Lord God, in the childbearing of Mary, you raised our human nature to the heights of heaven. Help us to live as a divine generation, and with her to praise and magnify your Holy Name. Amen.

Philip Barnes

Several hundred young people were gathered in a marquee in rural Norfolk. Again and again, they were told: 'You're gorgeous.' This wasn't a benefit concert for the 1990s pop group Babybird: it was the Walsingham Youth Pilgrimage. Philip Barnes, the shrine priest, wrote this prayer for the event, and a copy was given to each person at the end of a late-night liturgy.

Leave behind the insecurities that imprison you, the worries about image or self-worth. The incarnation of Jesus, the pilgrims were told, is the most astonishing reality of history because it involves you. The birth of Jesus is not the act of a God who deals with sin as a kind of hit-and-run job. Jesus does not slither out of his flesh, like a snake shedding skin, when the going gets tough.

At the incarnation, God implicated himself deeply in human history. The birth of Jesus has raised our humanity to the heights of heaven. In showing us the potential for the whole human race, he called us to live as a divine generation.

In seeking to end centuries of disagreement, the recent ARCIC report declared: 'Mary is in a unique way the recipient of God's election and grace' (*Mary: Grace and Hope in Christ*, Continuum, 2005). But, as always in the Judaeo-Christian tradition, the choice of an individual is essentially for the blessing of the wider community. God raised our whole human nature in the childbearing of Mary, through her 'Yes', which led to the normal joys and pains of pregnancy.

The incarnation shows us that God does not just use people. He requires the assent of our will – however faltering that may be. Often when we pray, it is hard to concentrate, or to find the right words. Yet, amid this cacophony, what God requires is our 'Yes' to his will for us; our conscious 'Yes' to allow him to love us further into life.

This isn't because God is a demanding control freak. Rather, it is because in allowing his will, we open up the drama of our lives to the transforming power of his love – the real extent of which we can only begin to imagine.

As we open up our time to God, he is able to use it not just for our own good, but also for the flourishing of those around us. It is no accident that, after the apostles received the Holy Spirit at Pentecost, they went out to the world to proclaim sight for the blind, healing for the sick, and freedom for all those imprisoned in guilt and despair.

So, living as a divine generation is not something for picture-book saints: it is our vocation now. The author of 1 Peter writes: 'You are a chosen race, a royal priesthood, a holy nation,' precisely because we are called to 'proclaim the mighty acts of him who called you out of darkness into his marvellous light'.

As she proclaims 'My soul magnifies the Lord,' Mary points us towards the essential human vocation. It is as we praise God, corporately and as individuals, that we are filled with the Spirit, who will enable us to be a blessing to those around us. The Acts of the Apostles shows us the infant Church gathered with Mary, constant in prayer, awaiting Pentecost. Gathered around the God-bearer, the Church receives the Holy Spirit for the same vocation: to be active God-bearers to the world.

In her childbearing, Mary is the pattern of Christian living. If we are content with a sanitized version of the incarnation, it is all too easy to forget that Mary was the first to worship Jesus, the first to feel his pulse, the first to discern his identity while his humanity was still being formed in the crucible of her womb.

She is one who praises and magnifies, because in sharing the intensity of his life with an illiterate teenage girl from Nazareth, God has irreversibly hallowed humanity. That's why 'You're gorgeous.' Don't forget it.

Jamie Hawkey

Wondrous birth

O Christ, whose wondrous birth
  meaneth nothing unless we be born again,
whose death and sacrifice
  nothing if thou be risen alone;
raise up and exalt us, O Saviour,
both now to the estate of grace
and hereafter to the seat of glory;
where with the Father and the Holy Spirit
thou livest and reignest,
God for ever and ever. Amen.

Eric Milner-White (1884–1963),
Dean of York Minster

Forget contemporary language. When it comes to a prayer such as this, it just doesn't modernize unless you compromise the estate of grace and tone down the seat of glory.

I recall the prayer at a courtyard service beside the Church of the Nativity in Bethlehem one Christmas Eve. It was a long-awaited moment: having been searched and interviewed throughout the daylight hours by 'security', I was cold, alone and utterly miserable, until I found myself invited home by local Christians, offered food, warmth, conviviality. I was moved to tears at the estate of grace.

As for the seat of glory: how do you picture it? This morning my toddler son clambered up to our oversized carver dining chair, and, with a smile of glee, sat back and stretched out his fingertips to claim each armrest. So I'm led to suppose a deep and luxurious throne, far too big for mortal beings, set at a table for a future feast.

This prayer presents a seasonal expression of the patristic formula I learned as a student: 'He became what we are, that we might become what he is.' Advent engages with the future part – our claim to the seat of glory. Then Christmas focuses the historical part. God's grace was poured into a tiny babe, whom we are invited to see and hold and embrace.

So often we join the chorus of complaint that Christmas has become so materialistic, forgetting how the chorus of angels was proclaiming precisely the same: that God had become material. 'See. To you is born this day a Saviour. Peace on earth.' The estate of grace.

When they heard this, the shepherds took off for Bethlehem. They followed the story, until they found themselves integral to it. Christ's wondrous birth brought about birth again in them. I spent Christmas in Delhi a few years ago, where I found people participating in nativity plays with the same spirit.

These plays were more than the sentimental enthusiasm of reception-class children (or their grandparents). They were about the imagination of adults – Hindus and Muslims, as well as Christians – keen to participate in the celebration and to choose a part in the drama. There were a few unusual roles, for sure. There was plenty of humour and certainly a freedom of interpretation. The effect was not so much a performance to relatives as an experience of the story first-hand – and, for some, a new birth.

So I pause to wonder where I fit into the story each time around. Having recently given birth myself, I'll be with Mary this year. Not, I fear, the traditional portrayal, poised in devotion and calm confidence. The Mary I project is excited but exhausted, shivering with the tension of private pain and future promise.

The drama in which I participate might embarrass the grandparents, so earthy is its materialism. I shall be tucking a nappy-changing bag behind the manger and discussing colic with shepherds and kings. Yet, also, I shall be tingling with joy at the midwife who has delivered a wrinkled, infant kingdom to the estate of grace, and promises hereafter an oversized seat of glory.

Jo Bailey Wells

Blessed Joseph

O blessed Joseph, happy among men,
in that it was given unto thee not only to see and hear
the God whom many kings desired to see and saw not,
   to hear and heard not,
but also to carry and embrace him, to clothe and protect him!
O God, who hast given unto us a royal priesthood:
vouchsafe, we pray thee,
that as blessed Joseph was found worthy reverently to hold
and carry in his arms thine only-begotten Son,
born of the Virgin Mary,
so thou wouldest make us in purity of heart and innocence
   of deed
to serve thy holy altars,
that we may this day worthily receive the sacred Body and
   Blood of thy Son. Amen.

From the Preparation for Mass,
The English Missal (1958) (shortened)

Every year, thousands of schoolboys are selected to play the part of Joseph in Nativity plays. It is a thrill for all children. Yet it is a role that challenges their teachers.

Scripture gives us some of the details of the carpenter's story: his genealogy, his reaction to Mary's pregnancy, his vision of Gabriel, his journey to Bethlehem, and his return via Egypt. We see a little of the home life of the Holy Family in Nazareth, and the anxious trip to Jerusalem when Jesus was 12. But we are given no words from Joseph's lips. He is in many ways a silent witness to Jesus.

Perhaps this chimes with the experience of many new fathers. In a delivery suite, there can seem to be an order of priority, however unintended: new baby, new mother, medical staff, new father. The same emotion must have been felt by Victorian fathers pacing the hall downstairs, and fathers of other generations.

Yet we know that such feelings, however understandable, are wrong. St Joseph's example shows us precisely how wrong. Joseph spent the four weeks before the first Christmas night guiding Mary and the Redeemer in her womb along the dusty roads of the Holy Land. Joseph it was who found the improvised delivery suite, and who was the only human midwife to attend her. Joseph was the first to see and worship his infant Lord, before even the shepherds arrived.

This prayer is one of the traditional prayers used in the sacristy before the priest goes to the altar. As Joseph saw, heard, kissed, clothed and watched over Jesus, so we do something similar in every eucharistic encounter. Jesus still enters our world in a tangible way. The priest's hands will hold the Body of Christ as once Joseph did. That tangibility may be a veiled one, but it is tangible none the less.

As we emerge from the font, and each time we return from receiving holy communion, we are all, in one sense, 'God-bearers', the title supremely used of Mary, the *Theotokos*. In his beautiful book *Redeemer in the Womb* (Ignatius Press, 1993), Professor John Saward reflects, 'The vocation of the Christian, inscribed in his baptism, is to mother the Son by obeying the Father in the Holy Spirit.'

The Christian also has a fatherly duty of care and faithfulness. St John of the Cross made the point that it was Joseph who first granted Mary and Jesus 'a home in his abode'. Joseph was called to be the guardian of the Word made flesh. His is a silent but powerful example that all Christians are called to emulate.

Kenneth Macnab

Easter

Light of the minds that know thee

O God, who art the light of the minds that know thee,
the life of the souls that love thee,
and the strength of the thoughts that seek thee:
Help us so to know thee that we may truly love thee,
whose service is perfect freedom;
through Jesus Christ our Lord.
Amen.

St Augustine (354–430)

'The light of Christ!' will sing out the deacon at the Easter vigil. 'Thanks be to God,' we shall cry. The celebrant will light the Easter candle, saying: 'May the light of Christ, rising in glory, banish all darkness from our hearts and minds.'

In our creation myth, God says 'Let there be light' (Genesis 1.3); in the temple, Simeon hails Jesus as the light to lighten the nations; the Fourth Gospel has Jesus say: 'I am the light of the cosmos' (John 8.12).

Use this prayer to acclaim God's light. We acknowledge the creative life that God as Creator and Father pours into the world, and seek 'through Jesus Christ our Lord' to enable that life to enlighten our minds, and give purpose to our lives.

Of course, the prayer does not mention the Easter Christ. But we know and love God through our knowledge and love of Jesus, whose resurrection from atoning death and burial we shall celebrate this weekend. We receive the gift of God's life through the resurrection of the Lord and the giving of the Spirit, mediated to men, women and children in baptism, eucharist and Christian fellowship. This active, seeking work of God to fulfil Easter in us inspires this prayer, and may inspire us so to pray.

The prayer's balanced lines act as steps up to the heights of the perfect freedom in Christ, which is God's destiny for struggling humanity. Its elegant composition is taken from the words of the great Father of the Church, St Augustine of Hippo. In its patterns, we hear the skills of the rhetorician and preacher. We hear him reminding us that 'the truth will make you free' (John 8.32). For that freedom we yearn and pray.

The prayer touches many levels. God in Christ seeks us at every level, but we may particularize his activity in us as light or life or strength, making himself present in minds or souls or thoughts of service. We might juggle the various elements in the wording, and use them as headings for reflection on God's work in our life, on our openness to that action, or our resistance to it.

But it is not intended to be a self-examination list. Its beauty is its lucid structure, in God travelling from light to freedom. I first became aware of this prayer in university days at college evensong, when it was prayed by the Revd Denys Whiteley, the Chaplain, who, everyone knew, was dedicated to a thinking faith and enlightened, useful lives. After 56 years, I am still grateful for it as part of the vocabulary of prayer. Without referring to them, it speaks of the hope of Good Friday and Easter.

John Gaskell

A *new vision*

O God our Shepherd,
give to the Church a new vision and a new charity,
new wisdom and fresh understanding,
the revival of her brightness and the renewal of her unity;
that the eternal message of the Son,
   undefiled by the traditions of men,
may be hailed as the good news of the new age.
Through him who maketh all things new,
   Jesus Christ our Lord. Amen.

Percy Dearmer (1867–1936)

Here is a prayer to pray in a troubled Church. It was composed by Percy Dearmer, who in his day was a well-known Anglican Catholic priest. He campaigned for the revival of English pre-Reformation ceremonial, and demonstrated it at St Mary's, Primrose Hill, in north London. He was co-editor of the *English Hymnal*, *Songs of Praise* and the *Oxford Book of Carols*, and a distinguished Christian Socialist. He wrote hymns – such as 'Jesus, good above all other' – and, while he did not quite make Poets' Corner in Westminster Abbey, he does lie in the North Walk of the cloisters there.

In this splendid prayer, we can offer to God his Church on earth, for Easter renewal. The Easter season recalls the resurrection appearances, through which Jesus, dead and buried and transformed through resurrection, himself transformed his friends into the apostolic Church, of which we are members now.

That calls us to the proclamation of the good news and the renewal of human life. Humankind's hopes of freedom, justice, and prosperity are met in potentiality by the resurrected Lord. Jesus instituted a new covenant, and each generation is called to live it out with renewal and reform for new times and circumstances.

Dr Dearmer's prayer, therefore, is one that we can aptly utter to God our shepherd, as we engage with the world of politics. What we are trying to do in our politics – whether we know it or not – is to forward God's rule and purposes of love; what Jesus calls the kingdom. As we pray this prayer, we make ourselves open to fresh expressions of the resurrection life, new things expressing national and Church renewal.

As Professor of Ecclesiastical Art at King's College, London, Percy Dearmer knew that the grand tradition of Catholic faith and practice needs fresh expression as times pass. It is 'defiled' by Christian timorousness about change, but, in the face of fear, the resurrected Lord can make himself known in change.

In St Matthew's Gospel (13.51–52), at the end of a long series of parables, Jesus concludes, 'Have you understood all this?' The disciples said yes, and Jesus said to them: 'Well then, every scribe who becomes a disciple of the kingdom of heaven is like a householder who brings out from his storeroom things both new and old.'

So instructed, we can pray for the blessings of a new age, and that the Church may be a sign of it. There is a particular value in the prayer's petition for 'understanding', at a time when so many Church problems arise from lack of it among brothers and sisters.

The prayer speaks to God of his son's message as 'eternal'. This reminds us that the noble goodness we recognize in Jesus as we read the Gospel is the incarnation of the truth of God, his word. Jesus's teaching and death and resurrection is not merely the focus of the faithful's devotion and the intended pattern of their lives – although it is that, and shapes the lives of millions – it is the very pattern of God's activity in human lives. It is an absolute for individuals, Churches and nations.

At the end of the Revelation to John (21.5), the one sitting on the visionary throne speaks: 'Now I am making the whole of creation new.' Of this renewal, the Lord Jesus is the agent – and men and women, in Church and state, are the ministers of it now: 'Your will be done, on earth as in heaven.'

John Gaskell

Promoting thy glory

Almighty God, the giver of all good things,
without whose help all labour is ineffectual,
and without whose grace all wisdom is folly:
grant, I beseech Thee, that in this my undertaking,
thy Holy Spirit may not be withheld from me,
but that I may promote Thy glory,
and the salvation both of myself and others.
Grant this, O Lord, for the sake of Jesus Christ.
Amen. Lord bless me. So be it.

Samuel Johnson (1709–84)

In this prayer by Dr Johnson, who could better the way in which the phrases of the opening address to Almighty God lead up to human 'folly'? Embodying the wisdom of his times, Dr Johnson had a profound sense of his own and others' sin and folly, and, as he turns to God for the Holy Spirit's inspiration, he is aware of the needs of all.

Perhaps – if one may dare to question – not all wisdom without grace is folly. Many wise men and women live and die wise, without faith and the grace that it brings. But, for the believer before God, human wisdom has the hope of redeeming grace. Enlightened by our Easter celebrations of God's foolishness expressed in the cross (1 Corinthians 1.25), and fulfilled in resurrection, we can absorb part of the great man's spirit by uttering his prayer.

Easter gives us participation in the communion of saints. We have good reason to be thankful for liturgical change, now that the Church of England calendar lists men and women, Anglicans and others, long revered by their fellow Christians, who are to be commemorated by the Church on earth. We join our prayers with them, and they with ours.

Samuel Johnson, moralist, has his commemoration on 13 December, the day he died in 1784. This day he shares with the martyr Lucy, the saint of light, not inappropriately for one who himself represented Christian, and indeed Anglican, enlightenment. Between 1750 and 1752, he published twice-weekly essays entitled *The Rambler*. Fame was yet to come from the great dictionary, then in preparation, which was published on

15 April 1755. He composed this prayer as he began the series of essays, to offer himself for God's blessing on the work.

The poet John Wain, in his profound and readable biography of Samuel Johnson (Macmillan, 1974), calls it 'a gravely moving prayer'. The use of it engages one with the deep seriousness with which Johnson lived his life in the sight of God, and his sense of our responsibility for the eternal good of our fellow men, women and children. As we pray this saint's prayer, we live some of his virtues: his deep compassion, his trust in reason, and his energetic pursuit of the will of God. John Wain remarks that his religion was not one of blazing vision and hosanna.

Dr Johnson's dictionary defines 'pious' as 'careful of the duties owed by created beings to God'. That was his religious attitude: as we pray his prayer, we are called to new thoughts about commitment, prayer, worship and service. If that sounds a bit like Lent, it is a way of living Easter, too.

We are reminded by the prayer that life's endeavours are the realization now – sometimes well, sometimes badly – of our final salvation in Christ. 'Amen. Lord bless me. So be it.' The ending speaks of a humble handing over to divine providence of Dr Johnson's – and our – hopes and fears.

Everything we do is done in the sight of God's eternity, a fact that brings with it our recognition of God's judgement, and our trust in resurrection life, revealed and shared by our Lord. And our lives are linked to others. So, as we come in prayer to 'Almighty God, the giver', we bring with us the Church and the world for salvation.

John Gaskell

Simon of Cyrene

Eternal God,
whose Son entered into his glory
by the hard and lonely way of the cross:
Give us, with blessed Simon of Cyrene,
to shoulder the easy yoke of Christ,
that sharing others' burdens,
we may follow in his footsteps
and enter into the mystery of his dying and rising;
through Jesus Christ our Lord,
who lives and reigns with you
and the Holy Spirit,
God for ever and ever.
Amen.

David Silk

Simon of Cyrene is an Eastertide figure. His story belongs to the Passion of Christ, but his commemoration day is 11 May. He reminds us that it is only through the window of the resurrection that we may fully enter into the meaning and mystery of our oneness with Christ.

Simon was in the wrong place at the wrong time. He was press-ganged by Roman soldiers to help Jesus of Nazareth carry the instrument of his own torture and death. Here, in the picture of two men yoked together by that cross-beam, is an image of what lies at the heart of discipleship of Jesus, and at the heart of the mystery of our redemption.

How the New Testament writers try, over and over again, to find some image that will lead us into this mystery: that the nature of Christian discipleship is that, like Simon, we share the cross with Jesus – we are united with Christ in his dying and rising.

We come to the cross to worship, to pray, to seek a clue to the mysteries of our life and death. But we are not one with the soldiers who are 'just doing their job' and are unrelenting; not one with the bystanders, who are only curious and sceptical; not one with the enemies of Jesus, who are scathing; not even with the faithful few who are puzzled and fearful.

We who are his disciples are on the cross with him, incorporated into him. The mystery of this is to be apprehended only when we accept that we can never relive the Passion of Christ. We can only commemorate and celebrate it, mystically and sacramentally; for we stand irrevocably on this side of the resurrection, and are irreversibly one with Christ in both his dying and his rising.

That link between cross and resurrection, between Passiontide and Easter, is always there in the liturgy of the Church. Originally, the great Paschal Vigil was a celebration of what we have now separated into Good Friday and Easter. In order to retrace our Lord's footsteps, to share his Passion, we have adopted a calendar and devotional styles that cause us to live in compartments. Simon spans the death and resurrection, and invites us not so much to go through it moment by moment with Jesus, as to glory in the cross and resurrection as one single mystery.

So it is that the allegory of the vine (John 15.1), or the metaphor of the bride and groom (John 3.29), are examples of the search for an appropriate way of expressing the union of the believer with Christ. This surely is what St Paul is on about in his constant repetition of the phrase 'in Christ'.

For many of us, it is possible to apprehend it more easily when we stand at the foot of the cross, hand in hand with Mary, who is his mother and ours (John 19.25–27). As she looked at him, she must have recalled the words of Simeon (Luke 2.35), 'a sword of sorrow shall pierce your heart'. Bone of her bone, flesh of her flesh: a mother could catch something of the mystery of being one with Christ in his dying and his rising.

We share the cross and resurrection of Jesus by baptism and confirmation (Romans 6.3–11); by helping others in need (Matthew 25.40); and by receiving help from others in their kindness (John 13.8).

Jesus calls us to be no longer servants, but friends (John 15.15), and, more than that, to be one with him. If we are to be his disciples (Luke 9.23–24; 14.27), we must take up the cross for ourselves: we must shoulder his yoke (Matthew 11.28–30). So we may say with Paul (Galatians 2.19–20): 'I am crucified with Christ.'

David Silk

Dysmas

O God, for whom Judas received the punishment of his guilt,
and the thief the reward of his confession;
Grant us the full benefit of your reconciling mercy:
that, as in his suffering and dying,
our Lord Jesus Christ gave to each his due recompense,
so he may free us from the sins of our old nature,
and bestow on us the grace of his risen life:
who lives and reigns with you and the Holy Spirit,
one God, for ever and ever. Amen.

Gelasian Sacramentary

In the early Middle Ages, there were three celebrations of the eucharist on Maundy Thursday: for the reconciliation of the penitents; for the blessing of the holy oils; and for the commemoration of the Lord's Supper. The penitents were those who had been put to open penance since the beginning of Lent, and were to be readmitted to communion for Easter.

Probably Gallican in origin, this prayer appears in the Gelasian and Gregorian Sacramentaries of the eighth and ninth centuries. It was adopted in the Sarum Missal, which was widely used in the Church in England until the sixteenth century. It survived in the Roman Missal until the revision of 1970.

The prayer is a relic of the liturgy for the reconciliation of penitents. It contrasts the penitent thief with the traitor Judas, and reflects on them in the light of the Lord's resurrection. As has been noted in connection with the previous prayer, that link between Passiontide and Easter is always there in the Church's liturgy, but we have adopted devotional practices that put the two in separate compartments.

At first sight, the penitent thief seems to be no more than an anonymous walk-on part in the story of the Passion (Luke 23.39–43). But tradition, from the apocryphal Acts of Pilate onwards, gives him the name Dysmas, which means simply 'dying'. He even has a commemoration day on 26 March.

'Remember me when you come into your kingdom.' Dysmas looked through and beyond the immediate suffering of the cross, rather as St John writes of the Passion and death of Jesus as 'his glorification'. Dysmas confessed faith in Jesus as the promised Messiah, and affirmed the hope of his return in great glory; and he prayed. His prayer was simply to ask Jesus to 'remember' him in his kingdom.

Reflecting the use of the word 'remember' in the Hebrew scriptures, this is a prayer that calls for care, pity, succour and salvation (cf. Genesis 8.1; 19.29; Psalm 25.7; Nehemiah 13.14, 22, 31). Nehemiah uses it three times to pray for himself. 'Remember me for good.' That is all it takes. The prayer is not cluttered and qualified by Nehemiah's feelings, ambitions and needs. All that is simply left to God. God knows all the circumstances and the secrets of the heart.

So, too, we may learn to pray: 'Remember me for good,' or 'Remember N for good,' naming someone. When we embark on prayers like 'O Lord, we know that . . .', we might well pause and ask ourselves what we are actually doing. If we would but pray without trying to educate God or those around us, or to coach God about what he ought to be doing, our prayer – and our lives – would be the more trustful and restful.

By contrast with Dysmas, Judas had betrayed Jesus. At the supper, Jesus had said to Judas, 'What you are going to do, do quickly' (John 13.27). Judas alone grasped the import of his words. Perhaps he knew, when it was too late, that Jesus could have washed him within, not just his feet.

Despite the three years of living in that little community of 12 men and five women around Jesus, three years of opportunity to glimpse the mind and spirit of the Master, Judas would be lost for ever. For whatever reason, he would do it his way. 'He immediately went out; and it was night,' writes St John (13.31) – the endless night of the soul who chooses self before God.

For Dysmas, there was a hope and assurance of resurrection; for Judas, only despair and darkness. Jesus, remember me . . .

David Silk

Sources and acknowledgements

The editor and publisher are grateful for permission to reproduce material under copyright. Every effort has been made to trace the copyright owners of material included in this book, and any omissions will be corrected in future editions on receipt of information.

Rubem Alves, *All Year Round*, British Council of Churches, 1987

Bible extracts are from the following versions:
   The Authorized Version of the Bible (The King James Bible), the rights
   in which are vested in the Crown, are reproduced by permission of the
   Crown's Patentee, Cambridge University Press.
   The New Revised Standard Version of the Bible, copyright 1989 by the
   Division of Christian Education of the National Council of the Churches of
   Christ in the USA. Used by permission. All rights reserved.

The Book of Common Prayer, the rights in which are vested in the Crown, are reproduced by permission of the Crown's Patentee, Cambridge University Press.

Rex Chapman, *The Glory of God*, SCM Press, 1978

Common Worship: Daily Prayer, Church House Publishing, 2005

Common Worship: Services and Prayers for the Church of England © The Archbishops' Council, Church House Publishing, 2000

Jim Cotter, *Prayer at Night*, Cairns Publications, 1983

The English Hymnal, Oxford University Press, 1963

The English Missal, Canterbury Press, 2001

Kathy Galloway, *Talking to the Bones*, SPCK, 1996

Stanley Hauerwas, *Prayers Plainly Spoken*, Wipf and Stock, 2003 (InterVarsity Press, 1999)

Etty Hillesum, *An Interrupted Life: The Diaries and Letters of Etty Hillesum 1941–43*, Persephone Books, 1999

The Iona Community Worship Book, Wild Goose Publications, 1988

The Lutheran Book of Worship, Augsburg Fortress, 1978

Alistair MacLean (ed.), *Hebridean Altars: The Spirit of an Island Race*, Moray Press, 1937 (Hodder & Stoughton, 1999)

The Methodist Worship Book, Methodist Publishing House, 1999

Eric Milner-White and G. W. Briggs (eds), *Daily Prayer*, Oxford University Press, 1941

Janet Morley, *All Desires Known*, SPCK, 1992, 2nd edn 2005

Janet Morley (ed.), *Bread of Tomorrow*, SPCK, 1992, 2nd edn 2004

Richard Nerurkar, in Steve Chalke (ed.), *Oh God . . . 120 Celebrities' Prayers*, Lion, 1999

J. Philip Newell, *Sounds of the Eternal*, Canterbury Press, 2002

Conrad Noel, 'The Crusader's Prayer', from the devotions of the Catholic Crusade

Frank Skinner, *Frank Skinner*, Century, 2001

Mother Teresa, *A Simple Path*, compiled by Lucinda Vardey, Rider & Co., 1995

Desmond Tutu, *An African Prayer Book*, Hodder & Stoughton, 1995, Bantam Doubleday Dell, 2000

Evelyn Underhill, *Eucharistic Prayers from the Ancient Liturgies*, Mowbray, 1964

Index of authors of prayers

Alcuin 136
Rubem Alves 178
Anonymous 12, 52, 82, 110, 118,
    122, 134, 138, 174
St Anselm 90
St Augustine of Hippo 194

Philip Barnes 188
The Venerable Bede 98, 172
Josephine Butler 126

John Calvin 100
Catherine of Genoa 38
Traditional Celtic 128
Rex Chapman 40
Pierre Teilhard de Chardin 16
Jim Cotter 170
Richard Crashaw 168

Percy Dearmer 196
John Donne 162
Francis Drake 154

Kathy Galloway 34
Arthur Gray 74

Stanley Hauerwas 70
George Herbert 148, 152
Etty Hillesum 10
Basil Hume 146

John Paul II 102
Samuel Johnson 198
Cheslyn Jones 78

John Keble 62

Alistair MacLean 14
Mechthild of Magdeburg 6
Eric Milner-White 104, 142, 190
Janet Morley 60, 144

Richard Nerurkar 156
J. Philip Newell 20, 22, 24, 96
J. H. Newman 130
Reinhold Niebuhr 86
Janet Nightingale 94
Conrad Noel 32

Jean-Jacques Olier 72

Alan Paton 88
St Patrick (attributed) 4, 26, 140, 158

Karl Rahner 58
St Richard of Chichester 142
Brother Roger Schutz of Taizé 42
Christina Rossetti 176

David Silk 114, 200
Frank Skinner 112
Robert Louis Stevenson 30

St Teresa of Avila 150
Mother Teresa 80
Leo Tolstoy 28
Desmond Tutu 36

John Wesley 64
Austen Williams 108